AF380737

Purloined Letters

**Psychoanalytical
Notebooks**

Issue 35, June 2020

Director of NLS Publications: Alexandre Stevens
Consulting Editor: Pierre-Gilles Guéguen
Editor in Chief: Janet Haney
Cover Image: Alasdair Duncan
Text setting & cover design: Linda Lundin
Translator: Arunava Banarjee
Proofing: Catherine Alexander and John Haney

Published by the London Society of the NLS
Correspondence Address:
Psychoanalytical Notebooks, 42D Maple Street, London W1T 6HF, UK
Email: janetrhaney@gmail.com

Copyright © Psychoanalytical Notebooks, June 2020

ISBN 9781916157620

Contents

Editorial

In the middle of editing these texts, I took a short break to watch a film, based on true events, about a group of men struggling to write (right) (wright) the end of a badly told story. They were doing it with the substance of their lives. The story begins on a terrible day in Vietnam in 1966. A strategic error sees a company of American soldiers walking into a well laid Vietcong trap and taking heavy casualties. Next, as a result of a tactical error, the American artillery begins dropping shells on these beleaguered men. A medical evacuation helicopter then arrives to airlift casualties out of the jungle, and, to cut a long story short, a young Air Force medic is lowered into the middle of the battle and saves more than sixty lives. He presses a love letter to his girl-friend into the hand of a wounded man who is rescued by the helicopter and who makes it back to the USA. Our medic doesn't make it home; the love letter is not delivered; and the paperwork that should have led to his posthumous medal is suppressed to save the honour of the officer who fumbled the overall planning of the operation. The main action of the story, thirty years later, sees this officer, now a US Senator, on his way to the top of the political heap, while some of the survivors of the disaster are still suffering profoundly and trying to deal with their pain and to get our hero the medal he deserved. The story is resolved when each of these "purloined letters" – the love letter and the paperwork relating to the medal – reaches its destination. It is only when the medic is assured of his medal in an official ceremony conducted at the very centre of his society that the wounded soldier is able to deliver the love letter to the woman for whom it was intended. Taken together, the "letters" organise the action that heals the wounds. They draw the threads to make a more manageable hole around which relations get reorganised and castration is accepted. As a result, each man manages to move on.

Such an examination of the film is made possible by Lacan's seminar on Edgar Allan Poe's "The Purloined Letter," which is placed (against chronology) as the first paper in the *Écrits*. The opening paper in the *Autres écrits* is "Lituraterre", and there are "many reasons", as Jacques-Alain Miller says in his prologue to that book, why it "seemed predestined to occupy" the same primary place. Each paper gives the orientation for reading the rest of each book to the letter. Similarly, each of these papers gives our current issue of the Notebooks its own compass points. The first of the three papers by Sophie Marret-Maleval collected here is her revolutionary reading of the life of a Frenchman who struggled to hold himself together by purloining a famous painting and forming a vital relationship with it. The third is her close reading of Lacan's landmark text "Lituraterre." The second paper in the series is a dissection of love and transference – questions vital to the psychoanalytical clinic. These three papers offer the reader an encounter with the letter of Lacan's later work. To read them is to experience something of the discourse of psychoanalysis as hewn by Lacan. By pitting your wits against them it is possible to reshape and renew the way in which you engage with life, literature, and practice.

Professor Sophie Marret-Maleval is an Analyst Member of the School (AMS) and a member of both the New Lacanian School and the École de la Cause Freudienne. She is the current director of the Department of Psychoanalysis at the University of Paris 8, the department established by Lacan himself in the 1960s.

Janet Haney
June 2020

The Purloined Picture

Sophie Marret-Maleval

The Purloined Picture

Sophie Marret-Maleval

In Lacan's last teaching, the Other is progressively reduced to its silence (following a trajectory which I will not develop here), i.e. to S($\cancel{A}$).[1] Pointing out the inexistence of the Other led Lacan beyond the logic of Oedipus. After defining the Name of the Father as the signifier that founds the law of language, the signifier of "the Other as the locus of the law,"[2] and as the one that "provides its support to the law,"[3] Lacan concluded that there is no such guarantee of the symbolic order; there is no Other of the Other. The invention of the object *a*, right from *Seminar X*, as that which has no name objects to the ordering power of the symbolic, as Miller points out, and therefore to the power of the Father, which comes up against the object *a* insofar as the latter resists the power of the signifier.[4] The paternal function will therefore be reduced. It will be displaced from the Other to the One, to the function of the master signifier, which is that of nominating the real. Evoking Genesis, Lacan underlines that naming "makes the dimension of what we call 'thing' appear, whereas things get grounded in the real alone."[5] Nomination, that is to say the connection between S_1 and a, between signifier and jouissance, will also be placed at the origin of the knotting of the real, the imaginary and the symbolic, the constituent dimensions of the speaking being. "*Nommer, que vous pourriez écrire n'hommer, nommer est un acte, d'ajouter une dit-mension*," says Lacan in *RSI*.[6] He equivocates on "*nommer*" (naming), writing it "*n*" apostrophe "*hommer*," with an "*h*," which could be read as "making a man," and which condenses nomination and becoming human. Language is what makes our humanity, it is what creates man.

Lacan goes on to say that naming is an act; naming is the act of adding a "*dit-mension*." This time there is an equivoque on dimension: he adds "*dit*," "the spoken," the dimension of what is said. In other words, naming adds the fourth dimension, that of knotting, by adding the dimension of what is said, which means that the act of naming is that of saying. It is the act of enunciation, that is, the action of the S_1 which produces the "spoken," or what is said, here consisting in the adjunction of a dimension (rather than the traditional dimension of utterance). The subject, by choosing to place himself as existing within the field of language, alienating himself to the signifier by saying, knots the three dimensions constitutive of the speaking being, correlating them to his saying. In that sense the three dimensions are correlative to each singularity, existing by and for one. Everyone has to find a way with them and knots them in their own way, be it borromean or not. The S_1 designates the speaking being as pure difference, it makes him exist as one, he makes the thing arise as real by inducing the loss of the object that causes desire and that governs his jouissance and around which his master signifiers revolve. Therefore, the knot will be borromean when the signifier and jouissance are connected by the phallus (the connection between the function of speech, i.e. that of the S_1 and jouissance, becomes its function in *Seminar XXIII*). It will not be borromean when this connection is not ensured.

The S_1 then occupies a major place in Lacan's last teaching. It is the signifier bearing the identification of the subject, reduced to the unary trait, to the fact of counting oneself as one, and of being identical to oneself only in that regard. It also has the function of a letter insofar as the impact of language – the institution of the speaking being – results in the loss of the object (the word is the murder of the thing). It makes the thing arise as real, following the function of nomination, but it has the function of an edge with the real, which enables the connection of the symbolic and the real. The function of connection is what allows for the knotting of the elements.

I'll try to explain this complex articulation by following Lacan's steps in *Seminar XXIII*, where he relies on Joyce's psychosis to push his construction in *RSI* and put it to the test.[7] Just as he redefined the psychoanalytical approach to psychosis with Schreber, he proceeds with a radical revision of the concepts of psychoanalysis and of his own contribution to it by teaching, via Joyce, that "paternity is a legal fiction."[8] Lacan starts with the fault of the knot and the possibilities of supplementing the flaw of the paternal function to give it a new interpretation. I will rely on Joyce's second epiphany to highlight the unknotting of the imaginary when the function of the S_1 is not put into play. I will then highlight the knotting function of nomination with the captivating story of a man who stole a Rembrandt.

The Unknotting of the Imaginary

I already commented on Joyce's epiphanies some years ago in London,[9] but felt the need to return to them briefly in order to make my point before developing the case of the art thief.

Joyce's epiphanies count as the first traces of his writing. They were simple notes at the beginning, from which he wrote short texts relative to what can be understood now as primordial experiences in his destiny, either in the form of memories or moments of perplexity. He then gave them the status of a poem, and later gave a definition of his epiphanies when he gave these vignettes a central place by using them to provide the narrative frame of his first novel, *Stephen Hero*, and then of his *Portrait of the Artist as a Young Man*, which led him to rewrite the initial version.[10]

I will analyse the second epiphany, which evokes, for me, the case of the man who stole a Rembrandt, in order to understand the effects of the detachment of the imaginary when the subject fails to be represented as a pure singularity by the S_1 and jouissance is therefore disjointed from language. Besides, the text testifies to Joyce's attempt to support himself with imaginary identifications and to correlate the pronoun that represents him to an image in order to give consistency to his being.

> No school tomorrow: it is Saturday night in winter: I sit by the fire. Soon they will be returning with provisions, meat and vegetables, tea and bread and butter, and white pudding that makes a noise on the pan ... I sit reading a story of Alsace, turning over the yellow pages, watching the men and women in their strange dresses. It pleases me to read of their ways; through them I seem to touch the life of a land beyond them to enter into communion with the German people. Dearest illusion, friend of my youth! ...In him I have imaged myself. Our lives are still sacred in their intimate sympathies. I am with him at night when he reads the books of the philosophers or some tale of ancient times. I am with him when he wanders alone or with one whom he has never seen, that young girl who puts around him arms that have no malice in them, offering her simple, abundant love, hearing and answering his soul he knows not how.[11]

Joyce remembers that when he was a child he used to evade the family atmosphere by reading fiction, as

Jacques Aubert notes. The narrator relives a scene in which, as a young boy, he crossed over the boundaries of fiction by identifying himself with ideal figures, embodied in the men and women of his history book on Alsace. What may appear as an ordinary identification with idealised figures nevertheless bears a trace of the subject's radical dissolution in the other when the master signifier fails to represent him as a singularity. Indeed, this text is striking because of the difficulty he encounters in understanding what it is about and, notably, in identifying the actors in the scene. The beginning of the text can easily be understood: the child ("No school tomorrow") is sitting alone by the fire, thinking. But soon his thoughts unfold into a list of provisions, and the ellipses let us imagine that it could be infinite. In the vignette, the metonymic movement of his thought betrays language's invasion by jouissance when the object is not connected to the S_1 by the phallus. This movement is interrupted, at the level of writing, by punctuation, the ellipses, which brings our focus back onto the reading child. Difficulties start with the sentence "Dearest illusion, friend of my youth!" Why is "friend" in the singular, and who is the narrator talking about? The first impulse would be to understand the exclamation "Dearest illusion" as an anaphoric mention of the characters of the book he is reading, but the singular mode prevents such an interpretation. To whom does the expression "friend of my youth" refer then? It must be understood that the illusion, the friend of his youth, is the image of

Joyce himself (the narrator) as a child reader. The text shows how Joyce, far from contemplating himself, relies upon an image of himself detached from himself, but which thus becomes that which represents him. As he puts it: "In him I have imaged myself." In him he has laid his image.

The subject of enunciation is radically severed from his self-image. If one may easily imagine a rather common scene in which the image of himself as a child accompanies the adult narrator in his thoughts, in his daydreaming, which could find its expression in a sentence like "he is with me when I wander alone," here, we find the contrary: "I am with him at night when he reads the books of the philosophers or some tale of ancient times." The materialisation of the body, of its image, lies on the side of the child, while the narrator is a purely abstract instance, disembodied, wandering, not assigned to a body, fluctuating, and it can lodge itself in the body of another, such as the men and woman of the story of Alsace. The flaw of primary identification is patent. The result is this paradoxical line "I am with him when he wanders alone," confirming the disembodiment of the narrative "I". The child reader is an image (an illusion) materialising the presence of the narrator within the world; he is the support of his phallic identification (it is the image that meets a woman). The narrator is supported in the present by this historicised image of himself as a child, an image constructed and extracted from the past. The vignette evokes the detachment of the imaginary, it bears its mark since it entails a difficulty in understanding easily the sense of the scene and thereby of the text, and to identify the characters. The sudden break between "I" and "him," and between the past and present tenses, blur our usual markers.

It becomes nearly impossible, in the course of reading, to correlate an image to a pronoun with certainty. We understand that the narrative is about fusion with the other because of the lack of assignment of the subject of enunciation to a body or to a place (which the reference to his wanderings also highlights). The text first seems to restore a distance between "I" and "him," between past and present, or even between the child and the characters of the story of Alsace, as the expression "Dearest illusion, friend of my youth!" might lead us to think. The word "illusion" evokes the lure of identification, but it also designates the image of himself, qualified as the friend of his youth. However, the narrative gets lost in the confusion of instances. If Joyce, through the narrative voice, tries to make a semblance of division happen, he only ends up with a paradox, "I am with him when he wanders alone," a logical impossibility unless "I" is a pure spirit, a disembodied mark. Finally, writing underlines how foreign Joyce's image is to himself. The text opposes "I" to "him," rather than making use of the reflexive pronoun "himself" (I am with myself).

Not only does the text deal with Joyce's failure to give consistency to the "I" or to represent himself by way of an image or of a signifier, and of the fragility of the knotting which depends on the function of the S_1 to represent the subject as one, but it testifies to this failure and reproduces it. Nevertheless, it points out how Joyce has tried to make himself be accompanied by an image of himself, placing his singularity there, by relying upon an external image of himself as a child that had the function of representing him.

More precisely, his epiphanies had the mission of representing him as traces or traits of his enunciation, as enigmas, i.e. to make the function of the S_1 emerge. They had to act as such with his first readers but also with other texts (the books in the library of Alexandria – the library burnt down during Antiquity – where Stephen reminds us in *Ulysses* that they were to be sent), or even with other signifiers, such as those in *Portrait of the Artist*, both trying to separate and articulate S_1 and S_2, as a reproduction of the movement following which the subject arises.[12] Joyce, says Lacan, relied upon writing to make a name for himself, thereby trying to knot the imaginary, as testified to in the vignette, which tries to correlate the subject of enunciation to the image of himself.

The Man with the Soap Bubble

The incredible story of Patrick Vialaneix echoes these Joycean phenomena relating to a precarious primary identification.

On 13 July 1999, in the evening, a priceless picture thought to have been painted by Rembrandt, *Child with a Soap Bubble*, was stolen from a museum in Draguignan. The picture shows the figure of a child, marked by sadness, holding a soap bubble in his hand. In spite of the amateurish nature of the robbery and the traces left by the robber, notably the hammer he used to commit his crime, the police could not catch him, and he kept the picture for fifteen years until, in 2014, he tried to give it back to the museum by means of a dubious transaction, and then gave himself up, causing general disbelief. In 2015, a documentary was made about this fantastic story, and was based on a striking interview with Patrick Vialaneix.[13] The latter died of a heart attack soon afterwards, in January 2015. Sylvie Matton, a novelist and art curator with a passion for Rembrandt, also wrote a well-documented fictional biography inspired by Vialaneix's own words, which gives access to some elements that shed further light on the logic of the robbery and of its consequences.[14] She focuses her narrative on Vialaneix's relationship with his father, whereas the interview highlights more precisely the support he found in the picture with regard to his identification. Sylvie Matton nevertheless reveals precious elements about his childhood.

Vialaneix's father, born in Algeria, was sent at the age of nine to a Jesuit boarding school in Algiers, where he was subject to a spartan education following military rules. He spent every summer there as well, never going back home. He remained there until he was eighteen and never crossed the threshold of a church afterwards. He left the seminary to commit himself to the OAS (the Organisation of the Secret Army, a clandestine organisation for the support of the French presence in Algeria) just before he took the final secondary school examination. He went in for "violent guerrilla warfare," according to Sylvie Matton. In 1962, his mother denounced him to the FLN (Algeria's National Liberation Front). Although he did not know who had betrayed him, he was informed that his life was threatened, and he flew from Algeria to France, where he had to do his military service, a period during which he was subject to harsh discipline because of his past. He was discharged due to heart disease, which he concealed from his wife, and for which he was operated on eight years later. Patrick, the third and last child, was born seven months after this first operation. His father became a manager in a bank agency, but he remained deeply marked by his violent past.

He insisted that Patrick's cot, when he was a baby, should be placed in a recess on the ground floor and that the door should be closed so that he would not hear him cry. Patrick and his two elder sisters were brought up in a military way; only the youngest sister seems to have been spared. Patrick, as the only son, was treated particularly strictly. Sylvie Matton wrote that the father would wake the children up at four in the morning to make them tidy and clean the house. She describes the violence of an alcoholic father, who drank in spite of his heart disease and told his children his war memories without sparing them the details, such as that of a young girl cut into pieces whose head he had fixed with tape to bury her, or the murder of an imploring Arab. He told these stories as a display of virility. He could be violent with his children. He destroyed Patrick's games and collections with an axe, reproached him for his bad results at school, and threatened to cut his throat with a knife for having eaten two squares of chocolate, until Patrick's sister confessed to having eaten them. He asked Patrick for forgiveness, but Sylvie Matton points out that Patrick lost all respect for him from then on. She relates his fascination with *The Enigma of Kaspar Hauser*, the film by Werner Herzog set in the early 19th century about a savage child who was secluded when he was young and was later found in a public square in Germany as a young man, looking crazed. There appears, discreetly, the fragility of his phallic posture which led him to consider himself as an animal and to identify with his dog.

Far from being trivial, his bond with his dog seems to have had a major function as the animal died only three months before the theft of the picture. The wolfhound, named Prince, had been adopted from a zoo to become a guard dog, a "real guard dog," as his father used to say. The signifier "guard" (*gardien*) took on a major importance for Patrick until he became the "guardian" of a Rembrandt. The dog was born in 1970, the same year as Patrick. He remained chained to a tree near his kennel, so, when his father was gone and when he did not go to school, Patrick would untie him and go to walk in the forest with him. His mother would turn a blind eye to these outings. Like Patrick, the dog was also subject to the father's violence. He would beat him to show "who the master is," forcing the children to witness the scene. Prince became Patrick's only confidant (sometimes he told him about his father's exploits during the war, for which he seems to have kept a certain admiration, putting the blame upon himself, following his melancholic bias). Patrick often shared his kennel. When they ran away to the forest, they would dig holes where they curled up together. Sylvie Matton underlines how Patrick would retreat from the world, cutting himself off from his father's violence, finding refuge by retreating into a bubble (recesses, holes, but also "language bubbles" since he would talk aloud to himself, as testified to by old family films. He probably addressed the dog in those moments. Later, he addressed the picture). His mother would say to him, "Here you are talking to your Jiminy Cricket again." In the documentary, Patrick uses the name of this cricket that embodies Pinocchio's conscience to speak of the child in the painting.

When the dog died, the father made his daughters bury it at night before Patrick woke up, and he did not tell his son. When he found out, Patrick made a small cross on which he carved Prince's name and then his own below, with the two capital Ps interlaced. He hung the cross on his birth bracelet where his own name was engraved. More than a confidant, the dog seems to have been a double, a projection of himself. His death robbed him of his self-image, $i(a)$, just as Lol V. Stein's ravishment leaves her deprived of any identification. Patrick's name, the signifier of his identification, is carved on the cross, testifying not only to the radical detachment of the image in which his identity had been laid down, but also to the fact that the foundation of identification, the function of the S_1, was affected.

From then on, Patrick started to speak to the plant that grew on the grave ten days later. It was a calamint. Then he started speaking to all the calamints growing at the edge of the forest, then to all the surrounding vegetation. He surrounded himself with a "benevolent microcosm," says Sylvie Matton, interpreting the child's passion for the picture as a way to defy death: "fixed on the canvas [...] the child will never die." The function of the picture for Patrick leads us towards another interpretation. Patrick got lost and scattered away in the silence of the Other. Language came loose when the image of his body was detached and identification failed to find a mooring for lack of a nomination – and of an orientation – thanks to the extraction of the object placed within the Other, whereas the subject came close to his identification with the object.

Then, three months later, when he was thirteen, Patrick came across the picture for the first time. Patrick was regularly taken to play football by his father, who pushed him to achieve highly in the sport and accompanied him to his training sessions and to matches. He was highly intrusive during the matches, which caused Patrick shame and exasperated the coach, who kept Patrick in the junior team in spite of his good results to keep his father away from the sports ground. Patrick's father had had a second heart operation three years earlier but he continued to drink and remained in a poor health. One day the father had flu, so Patrick's mother took her son to the match.

In her spare time, Patrick's mother had begun to paint in a studio six years earlier, which allowed her to have some distance from her husband. Patrick would help his mother, carrying the canvases and pots for her, stretching the canvases on the frames, and hanging the pictures on the wall for local exhibitions. Sylvie Matton reports that Patrick once asked her why she painted pictures that did not represent life, and why she used dark colours. She answered that the chaos of the colours expressed what she felt deep inside her. Patrick felt that her answer was abrupt.

After the match that day, Patrick's mother took him to the museum. "The first time I met the picture," Patrick says in the interview, as if he was speaking of someone.[15] Fifteen years after the robbery, his enunciation betrays the function of the picture for him. In the museum, he says, he was mainly interested in the suits of armour – they provided many corporeal envelopes where one could lodge oneself – and he took himself for a knight and started to play. When he arrived in front of the picture, and his mother showed it to him, he remembers her telling him, "He's a master." Indeed, the picture seems to have had the value of an identificatory image but in connection with the paternal function, holding value because of its author. The child and Rembrandt finally merge in Patrick's narrative, but we will come back to that point later. His mother explained the chiaroscuro to him, and we see that the picture also locates and veils the object, the gaze, to which Patrick was identified. "I looked at him furtively at first, and then his gaze captivated me," he says. Through this painting, his mother marked for him the sadness, the melancholy of the child. "I met myself in him," he said, associating on his unhappy life. He evokes "the sad and intense gaze" of the child, his "bubble about to explode, which will explode but we wonder when, just as life is going to end."

Sylvie Matton reports that his mother told him, "This child with his soap bubble on his hand looks just like you. See how Rembrandt's light gives life to him."[16] She notes that the full-face portrait seems to follow you with his eyes.

Although he did not see the picture again for four years, Sylvie Matton points out that it already had a specific function for him. She notes that Patrick would speak to it every day, as to "a friendly presence over his shoulder." While Patrick situates the moment when this dialogue began in a later period, the first address to an abstract child remains likely to have taken place much earlier, since the picture seems to have occupied the place left by the dog. Right from the first time he saw the picture he tried to find copies of it, but could not find any. He then relied on his memory of the picture. He could see it in the bathroom mirror by "orienting his face differently towards the window until the sun captures the bridge of the nose or the faint smile." The picture was an amiable image, contrary to Maupassant's "Le Horla". Patrick used to look for the play of light, and to induce it, in order to render the beauty of the picture. He became the picture. Was it another way of extracting and locating the gaze within an image? Patrick was occupied with the work of sublimation, "the celebration of the taciturn marriage of the empty life and the indescribable object," as Lacan says about Marguerite Duras's writing.[17] In his case, he celebrates the marriage of the image of the body (the empty life) with the object *a* (the empty life is also the signifier for Duras). Let's evoke Lol's strategy in the wheat field. She stands as the gaze upon the scene through which Jacques Hold takes off Tatiana's dress. He knows Lol is watching him, he is "the voice of the narrative," $; Tatiana is i(*a*), the image of the body, Lol the object *a*. Thus Lol tries to restore the knotting of the real, the symbolic and the imaginary, which came loose during the ball scene. She does it by occupying the place of the extracted object, the driving force of fantasy.

Regarding Patrick's attempt to restore the knot, the third instance, the symbolic, was probably made present thanks to Patrick's later conversation with the child. The child became his advisor, his Jiminy Cricket. Then Rembrandt took a place in the assemblage. Sylvie Matton notes that Patrick first avoided seeing the picture again in order not to be disappointed. He would think of the child, the projected image of himself, more than the picture. She underlines that, during that period, his academic standard deteriorated because he had trouble concentrating. At that time, bodily symptoms became more prominent. He sprained his ankle, which allowed him to stop playing football, much to the regret of his father, who mocked him and ran him down. Soon after, he began experiencing somatic pains for which he started taking medication, which he took to excess and abused later on. The fragility of Patrick's body image and of his phallic posture discretely appear here again.

Patrick had the occasion to see the picture for a second time when he was seventeen. His father had given him a motorbike and insisted that Patrick should go with him on a trip for several days. Every weekend he prepared for this trip, which his son dreaded because of his drunkenness. But Patrick did not dare to say no to him and thought of tinkering with the motorbike so that it would not start. The drunk father would fall asleep and forget about the trip when he awoke, only to start preparing again the next weekend. Somewhere between pride and terror Patrick went to the prefecture to get his registration papers. Since there was a long queue, he went to the museum. "There, I saw more than a child," Patrick says in the documentary. "I entered the canvas and I saw a friend. I started talking to him," he says as he evokes their "first discourse." Above all, it seems that the child started to talk to him too. Patrick tried to "get in touch with the canvas," and talked to it in a low voice, "as Don Camillo with Christ." He was "*my* Christ," the son speaking on behalf of the father. Patrick started to hear "advice, solutions, answers to my problems." It was "the beginning of a passion."[18] The child then became his confidant, as he told Sylvie Matton; the painting had become his Jiminy Cricket, his guardian angel. He started to take an interest in Rembrandt, and to gather documents about him. Patrick says that Rembrandt was "cast away by life," adding, "I liked that because I also felt like a castaway." Rembrandt is both a double and a paternal figure, as Patrick noted that he used to drink but also that he was a father who suffered from the death of his children.

Sylvie Matton relates another significant detail regarding the second time he saw the picture. Indeed, Patrick no longer had to stand on tiptoe to see the child. His eyes fixed on those of the child following a horizontal line. They stood on an equal level, which seems to have contributed to his projection into the image of the child.

She underlines that when he left the museum, he noted that a statue was missing, and he thought that one could steal objects from a museum.

The third time he saw the picture, Patrick was twenty-five. "It was more than complicity, a true exchange," "something magical happened with him." He tried to experience the same feeling in the company of others, but in vain. The wish to see it more often gradually crept in until the idea of the robbery arose. I wanted to do "something great," "to appropriate the picture," Patrick says, "to devise my own plan." I tried to render the equivocal nature of the French expression *"échafauder un plan de moi,"* since it means both to devise a plan by myself, and of myself.

The appropriation of the picture, of an image of the self, was what could invest him with power and greatness. The word "appropriation" must be understood literally as an attempt to incorporate, to restore, the detached image. To "appropriate" the image would mean to devise his own plan, a plan that comes from him, that commits him as a singularity, but also that distinguishes him as such, allowing him to delineate the outlines of the missing image. The issue of the knotting of the image is again attached to the restoration of his singularity, invested with the characteristics of value and greatness. Hence also the confusion between the child and Rembrandt: to "appropriate" the image is an attempt to restore the missing paternal function, that which sets up the function of the phallus. In *RSI*, Lacan specifies that the Father is the name of the name,[19] the one that puts the phallus into play (the second name). The phallus names maternal jouissance; it gives a name to the desire of the Other. The phallus is that which connects the signifier and the object. In Lacan's very last teaching the phallus and the S_1 are somehow confounded as signifiers that denote the subject and that name jouissance, or the phallus becomes a function of the S_1, that of naming jouissance. It seems that Patrick expected to have greatness conferred on him by the picture, which was meant to act for the master, Rembrandt, as a sign of him. It was thus meant to invest him with the characteristics of value and singularity, and it involved the recovery of the detached image. The object was thus caught within the image, named (as the chiaroscuro), extracted and located within the image as the medium of sublimation. Patrick's enunciation when he relates the theft bears the marks of this: "to climb the stairs, to cry out with relief, at last, I had it."[20] His narrative is littered with impersonal forms, here the use of the infinitive mood, which contrasts with the emergence of the "I" when he finally holds the picture.

It can be noted that the third time Patrick encountered the picture was at a particularly difficult moment in his life. He went through a period of massive consumption of antidepressants, he survived by working casual jobs, he tried to take his life after a broken romance, and he was imprisoned for ten months. He had used a shotgun in a punitive expedition against gypsies in the camp where his girlfriend's grandparents lived. Her son had come back with a burnt nose and a squashed finger because he had stumbled over a gas stove. Patrick thought he had been assaulted and hurt and left to avenge him. He was struck by his adversaries and threatened them with the gun to defend himself. The father of his partner involved the police but exposed Patrick in the process.

Sylvie Matton notes that the child and the painter were his only confidants while he was in prison. His father never came to see him as he could not stand the idea that his son should be imprisoned, feeling both shame and grief. Patrick seems to have kept in his mind the image of the child's sadness when he was arrested. He used to imagine that his father came to see him in secret, although his father had written to him that he had brought dishonour on the whole family. He would try to restore the lost honour by doing "something great." Let's note that his father was also marked by degradation because a client of the bank where he now worked had taken action against him for giving them bad investment advice. He was demoted for this.

Patrick never saw his father again. He died while Patrick was in prison, felled by a heart attack as he was chasing his mother in the street with a bat. Rembrandt embodied the one who had suffered from the death of his relatives and children, as Patrick had when the dog and his father died. His father's death plunged him deeper into depression. He seems to have accused himself of having disappointed his father by his absence. He could have changed the course of things by intervening. He had always been the one who stood between his father and mother or brothers and sisters, the one who got his father to calm down when he threatened to commit suicide. There, discrete self-reproaches can be discerned, the sign of the melancholic core of what appears rather more clearly as a schizophrenic position. Although there is no doubt about this subject's psychotic structure, there is no obvious triggering, his relation to the picture having probably contributed to maintaining his balance in spite of his instability. The theft of the picture seems to have played a part in normalising his psychosis, at least for a few years.

He saw the picture for the third time when he got out of prison and for the fourth time in May 1999, when, at the age of twenty-eight, he went to the museum to prepare the robbery. He seems to have secretly and gradually planned the theft throughout these years. Sylvie Matton notes that the child in the picture would tell him that the town should treat such a work of art better, and that he asked him to "come and take me."[21]

When he left prison, in 1995, Patrick resumed his massive consumption of medicines and had to be sent to a psychiatric hospital in February 1998 to get clean. During that period, he was hired by a company that installed burglar alarms; then, after detox, he set up a security firm. The imaginary identification with the guardian never ceased to accompany him, be it through his double, the support of his identification, the guard dog, or through the guardian angel (which the child embodied), his professional position, his relation to his father, his family and his friends (he went as far as to go to prison to protect his companion's child). The mirror relation to the other can feed on such reversibility. He became the guardian of the picture, and we will see at what price. His reliance on a signifier set in the place of a master signifier nevertheless seems to have compensated for the lack of a primary identification and to have oriented his existence.

In spite of the success of his security company, the idea of stealing the picture seems to have quietly crept in and become more and more urgent.

According to Sylvie Matton, Patrick seems to have justified his act by a desire for justice, revenge, and the rehabilitation of the Count of Valbelle – from whom the picture had been confiscated during the Reign of Terror in the French Revolution of 1789 – for his father, who had been mistreated as a child, and for Rembrandt, who had been harassed and robbed by the notables of his time.

Sylvie Matton evokes two triggering elements. In 1998, a few months before the theft, he met a friend, C., who acted as a paternal figure for Patrick, and thanks to whom he met his wife, after the robbery. The man used to give work to Patrick's company and contributed to boosting Patrick. Besides this – and this is probably the main reason that pressed him to act – four years after he came out of prison Patrick discovered that there were no pictures left of his father because, just after his death, his mother had left their house in haste, broke and leaving everything she had behind. She had disappeared for three weeks, seized by a strong desire for freedom, and debt collectors had come in her absence and taken everything away, including the photos. Patrick was angry with her, especially because of the missing family portraits. The theft has to be considered as a response to a new ravishing of his image and that of his father.

Patrick prepared the robbery down to the last detail. He dyed his hair in order to escape recognition and planned the theft to coincide with Bastille Day. This meant that the noise of the helicopters, out for the celebrations, drowned out the museum's alarms. He went inside and hid in a cupboard for six hours until the museum had closed and the staff had gone home. He had previously disabled the alarm system with a Stanley knife fixed to an orthopaedic cane and transformed into wire cutters. Only the alarm behind the picture rang when he took it off the wall. He wrapped the picture in a plastic bag and left without being seen.

He describes having felt a sudden, overwhelming euphoria for five or six hours. He placed the Rembrandt on a chest of drawers facing his bed and turned the light on and off to watch the chiaroscuro effect. "It was wonderful," he says. "I watched him, spied on him, I tried to talk to him but he did not answer, we took a picture of us." "Then I said: what did you do? You have robbed a Rembrandt from a museum." But, he adds, "I felt stronger, I felt grown up, I had done something great at last."[22] The theft of the picture is the reverse of the ravishing of his image when the dog died. It consists of the recovery of the image of the self. The act also singularises him and confers value on him: that of greatness. It puts into play a connection of the imaginary, the restoration of the S_1, which goes together with his naming as the guardian of the picture that gives him phallic value by making him "exceptional" and with a transfer of jouissance, a localisation of the object within the play of light on the picture. The knotting results from an act, which makes the subject arise as a singularity in his intimate relation to jouissance. It is an imaginary way of approaching the function of nomination, that of the Father, which he lacked.

Patrick left the hammer behind in the museum and was worried he might have left fingerprints, but the police forgot to take them when he was arrested and the fingerprints that had been taken when he was in prison were not integrated into the national database, as they should have been according to the law of the time. DNA sampling was not yet in use. Patrick escaped police inquiries and kept the picture for fifteen years.

Sylvie Matton relates that he wrapped it up at night and hid it behind the chest of drawers. He said good-night to him every evening. Gossips in the village and the press told of a romantic thief, courageous and bold. Patrick was flattered, his sense of self-worth improved, but he did not confess. The possession of the picture was much too precious.

He found himself to be confident in the future and in himself, and, she points out, he would relive the theft in his thoughts. The need to see it became less urgent since he had the picture. Its presence was enough. He would look at it sometimes in the evening, or during the weekend, observing the play of light on the picture. At that time, he met a woman through his friend. He says that he had become "self-assured, positive, protective, enthusiastic." Nevertheless, he did not reveal the presence of the picture, which she only discovered fifteen years later. "I formed a clandestine relation with it, it was my greatest lie," he said. Sexual relations with his partner seems to have aroused a more urgent need to see it. This probably weakened his phallic posture, and so he devised excuses in order to make time for it. When they lived together, he would take the picture out when she was away. "Our meetings were shorter but more impassioned," he said. When they moved, she asked about the parcel, and he said it was a picture of his father painted by his mother. The subject of his father was taboo, so she would never ask to see it. Sylvie Matton also notes that she was afraid that she might not like the picture and that Patrick would insist on its being hung. "I was never tempted to tell her, it would have destroyed things, feelings," he said. The picture harboured the most intimate part of his being and it was probably necessary that it should be only for him.

When his friend died, he felt like an orphan and went through a very difficult period. He asked for the disability pension that had been offered to him nine years earlier. It is also the moment when his partner, who was accommodated by this friend and then evicted when he died, moved in with Patrick. It became more and more difficult to be away from the picture. He never wanted to sleep away from home, and he hardly left his flat as he had to "keep him, to watch over him." "I had to take care of him, I was his guardian," he said in a radio interview.[23] Since his girlfriend worked far from their place, she was away for part of the week and so he had to discipline himself and limit his exchanges with the child to three hours a day, Sylvie Matton relates. Then his girlfriend got pregnant. One day, as they were coming back from Patrick's mother's house, where they had gone for lunch, they discovered they had been burgled. The Rembrandt, hidden under the bed, had been spared. Patrick was relieved, and his partner was surprised that he should think so little of the burglary. They missed a Rembrandt, he says with pride and amusement in the documentary,[24] but the burglary nevertheless marked a change. He had failed in his role as the guardian of a Rembrandt, Sylvie Matton notes. The picture could have been stolen. It was "difficult to guard," Patrick underlines in the radio interview. Suspicion crept in, he felt persecuted by the neighbours, watching for the slightest movement outside his house. He wanted to leave the South of France, but his girlfriend was about to give birth and she delayed moving. Patrick slept in the living room to prevent any attempt at a break-in. He was soon to become a father, which probably contributed to this paranoid watchfulness, and reinforced the imperative of being the guardian of the child.

Sylvie Matton notes that he looked for photos of the painting in order to use them during his girlfriend's maternity leave, since she would be at home every day, which would give him less time with the picture. But all he could find was the photo published in the newspaper at the time of the theft. The birth of his son, named Robin, after Robin Hood, did not calm him down.

Three weeks later his motorbike was stolen. They decided to move. They settled in the Lot et Garonne, in the countryside. But Patrick realised that the house was infested with termites. He was frightened for the picture, fearing "that it would crumble away under his fingers," and so they moved a second time. Their son was three. Patrick was increasingly subject to bodily symptoms, such as backache and stomach ulcers, and the presence of the picture became more and more important to him. However, after settling into a new house and their marriage in 2005, a short period of relief followed. Patrick even thought of qualifying as a sports teacher to train young boys in football, something he had started doing in a place nearby. He could leave his house for short periods and even agreed to go to Amsterdam for their wedding trip. When they came back, however, he took the picture out of its cover and saw that a coin, which he used to catch the light, had become oxidised. In the documentary, he adds, "the nails were covered with verdigris." It was then that a new period of obsessive fear began. Sylvie Matton says that he thought the child had felt betrayed because he had left him to go to Amsterdam. Using his son's asthma as a pretext, he forced them to move a third time. The picture was never safe enough, he says, evoking his "paranoia." They settled in a new house, in the woods, where their second son was born. His wife speaks of the triggering of his phobias at that time: when he left the house, he would come back two or three times to check that the doors were closed, he would unplug everything, "his obsessions had taken over all family life." They could no longer go on holidays. In the documentary, he says that he could see that his wife's behaviour was changing! "We quarrelled" more often" he said. He measures what happens to him through the other, as in a mirror. My life was "asphyxiated," he says.

Sylvie Matton describes how Patrick had to go to hospital for a routine operation, which turned out badly because of blood poisoning and morphine-induced hallucinations. He then feared that the child could be an "evil spirit," and he would repeat to himself, "The child is love incarnate," but seeing that he could die, Patrick concluded that he could not keep the picture any longer.[25] Patrick explains that he decided to give the picture back because he was suffocating, but the documentary cuts these developments. "For fifteen years, I spent my life admiring him, cherishing him," "but there, my decision was firm, I had to give him back."[26]

He did not know what to do. "Going to the museum and handing the picture back saying 'I am the thief who stole the Rembrandt' seemed difficult. How do you give a Rembrandt back? It was not written." Patrick spoke to a friend who told him about insurance companies that took stolen works of art back, allowing him to imagine that it was a legal procedure and that he would be rewarded. He wanted the picture to be handed back to the museum. He met the so-called insurance company and was paid with a cheque which he never cashed. He says that as soon as the picture was gone, "it was the end of the story and the beginning of a new life."

The police department that specialised in stolen works of art learnt that the fraudulent sale of a Rembrandt was going to take place. They suspected that it could be the picture stolen from the museum in Draguignan and caught the suspects in action. Patrick learnt about this in the newspaper. "*I* was the thief, the only one," he says, underlining how much he was concerned with being recognised as the author of the theft, the act which granted him singularity and greatness. Patrick decided to give himself up. He relates that on 19 March 2014, he called his wife and said "Please come, I have something important to tell you" and he told her: "When we met there was a theft, I am the thief." He speaks of her silence: "What was to be said, what was to be done? It was too late anyway." "It was the most painful moment we had to face." His wife understood that she had shared her husband's love with a picture stolen fifteen years ago. She went with him to see a lawyer. The latter did not believe him at first but she had to recognise the facts. Patrick "*had* talked to the picture for fifteen years." Due to the statute of limitation of three years for theft, he was not sent to prison as he believed he would be. "Imprisonment was inevitable, *I* was the thief," he says. Nevertheless, he had to be prosecuted for the possession of stolen goods, criminal conspiracy, and the laundering of dirty money, of which he was suspected after the sale of the picture. In the radio interview, Patrick says he felt "liberated ever since giving the picture back." He had been "the guardian of the picture for fifteen years." "I suffered from guarding him," he said. He felt "happy that his story would be published in a book," "to say what really happened," and he wanted to be "invited to the exhibition for the return of the picture, to see it again." The interview testifies to his pride rather than to any guilt. However, a few weeks after the picture was back in the museum in Draguignan, on the night of 20 January, Patrick died of a heart attack. "Once he had given the picture back, *he* passed away," his wife says, "The child with the soap bubble and Patrick were as one."

With the theft of the picture Patrick tried to recover the missing image, first placed in the dog as his double, then stolen from him and unknotted when the dog died. The specific feature of the picture was to represent him, with the trait of phallic value conferred by the greatness of the painter (and his value in the eyes of his mother). The picture also allowed for a localisation of the gaze; a fastening of the object. Besides, the theft participated in conferring singularity on Patrick by making him exceptional and it contributed to inventing an imaginary nomination (the guardian of the picture) as an echo of the first imaginary identification with the guardian dog. However, the difficulty of fulfilling this role, due to problems related to the preservation of the picture, and the possibility of its being stolen, increased the frailty of the knotting, contributing in turn to the unbearable situation, and to the restitution of the picture, but probably also, to Patrick's death. With the picture, Patrick put into play the elements participating in the borromean knotting by the sinthome, by the function of nomination: the fastening of jouissance, an imaginary approach of the S_1 (by the signifier "guardian" and the value attached to the theft), as the S_1 has the function of representing the subject as a singularity, and the function of fastening the object, connecting signifier and object (here the object is caught and located within the image). A similarity with Joyce can be noted by the fact that both tried to support the image of the self with an external image representing the subject. Joyce used the vignettes of the epiphanies to represent himself as an author in the same way. Inserting them within *Portrait of the Artist*, he knotted them to the imaginary dimension of meaning, contributing to a kind of autobiographical writing that made of his portrait the paradigm of the artist.[27] Jacques-Alain Miller remarks that, for Joyce, writing made a symptom out of the humming of language (as language had started to hum with echoes), and enabled the writer to make a name for himself. Writing was a way of trying to knot the detached imaginary, thus supporting his singularity and fastening his jouissance.

Epilogue: in the documentary, Patrick's wife says she would like to see the picture in the museum ... to find answers.

Lecture given in English at the London Society of the NLS, 8 June 2019

Transference Reveals the Truth of Love: Love and Transference in Lacan's Last Teaching (...*or Worse, Encore, Seminars XXI and XXIV*)

Sophie Marret-Maleval

Transference Reveals the Truth of Love: Love and Transference in Lacan's Last Teaching (...*or Worse, Encore, Seminars XXI and XXIV*)

Sophie Marret-Maleval

The notion of transference evolves throughout Lacan's teaching and becomes progressively detached from the imaginary register. From the beginning it is linked to love. Transference is then considered as an obstacle to the analytic experience. While promoting the symbolic, transference love becomes the driving force of the cure. Finally, the analytic experience is itself considered in the light of love, which implies a renewal of the notion of love and therefore of transference. It is no longer a means but an effect of language, of analytic experience, becoming, while identified with love, the analytic experience itself.

Indeed, the notion of love is promoted and pushed forward in Lacan's last teaching. All occurrences of the notion of transference appear to be linked to love until Lacan claims: "Transference Reveals the Truth of Love."[1] We will try to understand this link in Lacan's last teaching and to see what has become of the notion of love and of transference.

From the Imaginary to the Symbolic

In 1951, in his "Presentation on Transference," Lacan identifies transference as the emergence within the progress of Dora's cure, in a moment when the analytic dialectics stagnate, of the "permanent modes according to which she constitutes her objects."[2] That is to say that the feelings of Dora are crystallised onto the person of Freud, transferred from Mr K to him, and Freud remains too much identified with Mr K to be able to interpret the transference correctly, says Lacan, thus blocking the progress of the dialectics of the cure (its logical unfolding). The imaginary becomes too present, contradicting the symbolic, the logical process of analytic experience. Transference is linked to this surge of the imaginary in the foreground. Lacan follows Freud, for whom transference "goes on *invisibly* behind the progress of the treatment." It is a driving force and an obstacle because it is limited to the imaginary projection onto the person of the analyst of the feelings of love and hatred experienced by the patient, in this case Dora.

But Lacan also considers that this surging of the imaginary is linked to Freud's counter-transference. He has put himself too much in the place of Mr K, interpreting Dora's answers as an avowal of her love for him, missing the importance of Mrs K in her scenario. Again, the imaginary presents itself as an obstacle. The appearance of transference on the analytic scene, the overwhelming presence of the analytic couple, of the patient's feelings towards the analyst (negative transference in the case of Dora), is a sign that something remains unanalysed. Transference is somehow already linked to love (and its opposite) and to the appearance in the foreground of this projection of feelings, of emotions, that usually runs invisibly, as a condition of the cure. The cure must lead beyond this crystallisation, this projection, which has to be dissolved to reach the truth of the symptom.

Lacan asks: "What then does it mean to interpret transference? Nothing but to fill the emptiness of this standstill with a lure. But even though it is deceptive, this lure serves a purpose by setting the whole process in motion anew." Transference has to be interpreted. Imaginary constructions have to be appealed to in order to make the imaginary lose ground again to the benefit of the logical process. Love and transference are already closely linked but on a strictly imaginary plane, contributing to the process of the cure but also objecting to it.

Although Lacan links transference to the imaginary, it is also part of the logical process of the cure; it is part of its driving force. Lacan will thus progressively consider transference on the level of the symbolic, making its function even more essential as it is detached from its imaginary effects (expressed feelings for the analyst).

Transference thus becomes more clearly connected to love, while love itself finds a symbolic expression as a metaphor. Transference *is* love in the sense that it finds a similar articulation. The subject addresses the analyst, the Other, in order to understand the cause of his suffering. He puts his lack forward in search of completion. The analyst must unveil, beyond the demand for knowledge, the lack in the Other, and the lack of an imaginary answer and possible completion of the desire of the subject. Transference reveals the true nature of the patient's quest, the irrecoverable object of desire, which constitutes its incentive and which is the true driving force of the cure. He can but meet and accept his own lack. Lacan will later formalise the object of pursuit as the object a – the object that causes desire – a real one in which a lost jouissance is located. An object is extracted and placed in the Other, which becomes the driving force of the subject and of transference. In his seminar on transference, Lacan thus links transference and love again. The logical metaphor of love is equated with the process of transference. Love is correlated to a lack within the subject caused by the fact that he is a speaking being, the subject of language. The word is substituted for the thing in its absence. The word is "the killing of the thing."[3] The subject of language is marked by a fundamental want to be; the subject is marked by a lack ($) and is what a signifier represents for another signifier, meaning that the subject is never represented within the signifying chain but between the signifiers as the source. This produces the One, the enunciative instance to which meaning is related, and which literally *makes* sense.

The metaphor of love relies on the substitution of the *desiring* one (the one who sets his partner in the place of the desired object) for the *desired* one. What is desired is the desiring one in the other, which can only be done if the subject is placed as desirable. The demand for love stems from the gap in the Other.[4] It is a demand to be loved, but its aim is being; it aims at obtaining the supplement of being which we lack, namely, "what slips away most in language." "Language imposes being upon us," Lacan says, "and obliges us, as such, to admit that we never have anything by way of being (*de l'être*)." In his partner, the subject is looking for the semblance of being that is supposed as object *a*. Lacan also explains, in *Encore*: "Doesn't the extreme of love, true love, reside in the approach to being?" Thus, love aims towards an object that is a "substitute for the Other," and from which jouissance depends, which causes it. We will come back to this later.

The metaphor of love is the process of substitution whereby the subject tries to reach the object of desire within the Other, but he wants to be desired, and aims at a reversal according to which he becomes the object of desire.

Transference thus also differs from love because, in love, the loved one is meant to answer back. When this reciprocity of the metaphor is blocked, when the analyst does not answer the demand for love, the analytic experience leads to the acknowledgment of one's impossible completion, of one's lack, and of the true nature of the object at stake. Lacan can thus point out paradoxically that love is always reciprocal because the desire of man is the desire of the Other, as he put it in *Seminar V*, making it clear that desire is the desire for a desire – a desire to be desired – and that desire is contingent on the supposition of a desire within the Other; hence, its flaw and its lack. The aim of transference, of the analytic experience at that time, was to acknowledge one's desire and, therefore, oneself as a desiring subject, liberating oneself from one's imaginary bearings.

"What Makes Up for the Sexual Relation"

Transference and love are brought close together again in *Encore*, as the notion of love is again revised. Love is "what makes up for the sexual relationship," the sexual relation, which does not exist. The inexistence of the sexual relation is at the heart of the last Lacan.

In *Seminar VI, Desire and Its Interpretation*, Lacan had gone a step beyond the belief in the supremacy of the signifier, which led him towards the invention of the object *a* in *Seminar X, Anxiety*. There he makes it clear that what lacks within the Other is not a signifier, the phallus, as he had claimed until then, but a real object, i.e. something radically heterogeneous to the dimension of language, of the Other. The power of language upon the real is thus put into question since the Other has no hold on the real. The object is without a name, as Jacques-Alain Miller points out; therefore, it is what questions the supremacy of the Other.

Jacques-Alain Miller notes, however, in "Six Paradigms of Jouissance," how, up until the last teaching, jouissance remains discursive. It circulates within the signifying chain, falls into a system, as the four discourses testify, since the object *a* operates within a set of logical relations. Lacan goes as far as the "posing of a primal relationship between the signifier and jouissance," considering that "the signifier represents jouissance,"[5] between S_1 and S_2, rather than the subject (the subject was primarily defined by Lacan as what the signifier represents for another signifier). *Seminar XVII, The Other Side of Psychoanalysis* is the turning point of this conception. With *Seminar XX, Encore*, there is an inversion regarding the whole development of Lacan's previous teaching. "Lacan, truly, cuts the branch on which all his teaching was sitting, and there will be, in the final part of his teaching, an attempt to build another conceptual apparatus out of the debris of the preceding one," says Miller, who also points out that this new paradigm is that of the non-rapport. Where the function of language, and of the structure, was to "capture [...] the living being, the organism," the non-rapport appears as the limit of the grasp of the structure upon the real. Speech is no longer understood as communication but as jouissance. "Whilst jouissance was, in his teaching, always secondary by comparison with the signifier," Jacques-Alain Miller underlines, "[...] language and structure hitherto treated as primordial givens must now, in this sixth paradigm, appear as secondary and derivative" (PN34: 64). The articulation S_1–S_2 (i.e. meaning) becomes secondary by comparison with $S_1 a$ (i.e. the mark of the signifier upon the body), so that Lacan will ultimately privilege the notion of the sign over the signifier and claim that the signifier is the cause of jouissance.

Love is the "sign that one is changing reasons," is changing discourses, says Lacan in *Encore*. He connects love and the sign – love as a sign – which is not included within the structure of the discourses. The sign leads towards another logic from that of the logical relation upon which the structure of the discourses is built. The sign is linked to the letter, a displacement of the notion of writing, which has to be situated with regard to what does not cease not to be written, i.e. the sexual relation.

"Does love consist in the fact that what appears is but the sign?" asks Lacan. Love is the attempt to create a link between $\$$ – which becomes S_1 in *Encore*, when Lacan points out that the subject is One, only represented as one and as a lack by an asemantic signifier – and the object *a*. The sign represents something for someone in Peircean logic. Lacan says the smoke is the sign of the smoker; the sign connects object and subject, it is the junction of two dimensions that have no part in common (the signifier and the object). In that way, love is a sign and, indeed, common experience testifies to the fact that love is a matter of signs: of signs of love. Lacan points out that "love in philosophical discourse aims at being," which is "what slips away most in language," being reduced to object *a*.

Jacques-Alain Miller notes in the last paradigm that "the concept of language, the earlier concept of speech as communication, as well, the concepts of the big Other, the Name of the Father, and the phallic symbol are all pushed to the point of collapse into semblants" (PN34: 64-5), which means that they are no longer primary, structuring fictions, but secondary fictions. The notion of semblant also means, however, that these terms are situated between the symbolic and the real, hence their reduction "to a function of stapling together elements that are fundamentally disconnected." The Name of the Father, for example, knots the three elements of the borromean knot; it is reduced to the connection S_1a, to a function of nomination, that of naming the real. It works as a "letter" and it is this primary function as a connector that enables the knotting of the symbolic, the real and the imaginary. In the same way, the phallus names the jouissance of the mother, and acts as a connector between the sexes. "All the terms that, in Lacan, provide connection – the Other, the Name of the Father, the phallus – which used to appear as primordial terms, even as transcendental terms, since they condition all experience, are reduced to being connectors," notes Miller.

The notion of connectors that write a logical relation has to be grasped through the background of the non-rapport. They belong to the same paradigm, the same logic. Miller makes clear that "this paradigm is based essentially on the non-rapport, on the disjunction – the disjunction of signifier and signified, the disjunction of jouissance and the big Other, the disjunction of man and woman under the heading

There is no sexual rapport. This is truly the *Seminar* of the non-rapports."

He explains that whilst the notion of structure implies that these terms have a transcendental function, "coming from an autonomous dimension, and prior to experience and conditioning," with the last teaching "we have the primacy of practice. Where there was transcendental structure, we have pragmatism, and even a social pragmatism." The non-rapport is therefore a concept "to be put against that of structure." He defines structure as "the formulation of relations in the plural to which, without more thought, we give the quality of being real on the grounds of necessity, that is to say, that which never stops being written." "This Seminar *Encore* opens up a new kind of relation that limits the structural empire," that of the non-rapport, shaking the series of constituent "relations" of the previous paradigms (notably the link between S_1 and S_2, the paternal metaphor). Lacan's last teaching points out the fundamental part played by "what does not stop not being written," i.e. the sexual relation, as Lacan formulates it.

There Is No Sexual Relation

In *...or Worse*, Lacan specifies that "It is with Φ (the symbolic phallus) [...] that everyone has rapport."[6] There is no natural relation between man and woman because sexuation and sexuality are only relative to the signifier, and more specifically to the phallus, as an intermediary between the sexes. It is that which vectorises sexual jouissance, from which it stems, as Lacan puts it in *Encore* (it stems from traces upon the body, the phallus as a mark), although the jouissance of the Other does not depend on it (it depends on the object *a*, which causes it). He adds: "Phallic jouissance is the obstacle owing to which man does not come [*n'arrive pas*], I would say, to enjoy woman's body, precisely because what he enjoys is the jouissance of the organ." On the one hand, man only approaches the Other sex by means of the phallic signifier (the signifier of sexual difference), which Lacan relates to the secondary sexual characteristics [*caractères sexuels secondaires*] which he considers as traces upon the body, while making it clear that "nothing distinguishes woman as a sexed being other than her sexual organ [*sexe*]" (in the sense that the phallus signifier is the organ). He further notes that jouissance is fitted out [*appareillée*] by language and that "reality is [only] approached with the apparatuses [*appareils*] of jouissance." In other words, the phallus is one of the apparatuses of jouissance, the use of which is to approach the Other sex. However, he also makes it clear, in *On a Discourse That Might Not Be a Semblance*, that the phallus in not a "medium" for all that, because on the side of women there remains something unknown that cannot be named. On the other hand, men only approach the Other sex by putting the phallus at stake, as that which makes a man of him and, therefore, that which he enjoys. "Jouissance, *qua* sexual, is phallic – in other words, it is not related to the Other as such," he adds.

Besides, Lacan prolongs the logical construction of his assertion "there is no sexual relation" by determining the consequences of the specificity of the phallus as the only signifier of sexual difference, as well as those of the lack of a signifier for Woman, by specifying the relation of the notion of "relation" to the dimension of logical writing.

He explores the paradoxes of negation by first showing that non-x is equal to infinite space. Starting from this statement, he will rely upon the "theory of sets" to underline the dissymmetry between men and women. If man and woman can only be defined by the intermediary of the phallic signifier, then there is no signifier for Woman; there is no specific signifier equal to the phallus for women. But Lacan will not be content with a definition via the negative. Women are not non-men, and precisely, the negation opens up onto an infinite space, i.e. onto the absence of a nomination for non-men; onto the absence of a closed set defining a universal of the type "all women." Lacan points out that women are not-all within the phallic function, that a part of their jouissance is not correlated to the phallus, but to the lack of a signifier to name their being. He postulates that women enjoy a supplementary jouissance, which is linked to this specific lack of being, a jouissance of a lack of being, of a lack of name. He makes this point clear with the theory of sets by distinguishing the One of the element from the One of the set. To close a set, a collection must be formed that can be gathered under the same signifier. However, it is the One of the set that lacks for women, which makes it impossible to close the set of women. It is therefore the reason why the set of women is an open one and cannot be closed; it is infinite. The phallic signifier cannot be the One that would constitute the set as a closed one, that would name it or define its borders. Thus, women are not-all subordinated to the phallus. Lacan rather defines the feminine position in relation to the lack of a signifier to name her being.

With the not-all, Lacan also introduces a kind of infinite that somehow makes a hole in the all. Jacques-Alain Miller in "Le partenaire symptôme"[7] represents the not-all by a hachured square inside the set of the all, on the border of this set, designating a limit within the all, and underlining the specificity of the not-all which consists in subverting the all. Thus, the not-all becomes generalised in Lacan's last teaching when Lacan lays the stress on a not-all phallic jouissance, a non-Oedipean jouissance, at the level of the sinthome, when he definitively breaks away from an Oedipean perspective.

Thus, the jouissance of women is divided between phallic jouissance and feminine jouissance. On the one hand, a woman expects a supplement of being from a man, a nomination. Her jouissance aims towards the phallus, understood as the signifier that the Other lacks. Hence the fact that women want men to talk to them, to name them as exceptions, to give them a nomination within language. On the other hand, women enjoy this very lack of a signifier to name them, i.e. S($\not{A}$) – the "signifier of A inso-far as the latter is barred." They enjoy the lack of a signifier within the Other which is a properly feminine jouissance.

As for the set of men, it is closed. The phallus is the signifier which provides the One of that set, which makes it possible to say "all men," to define a universal. However, Lacan also relies upon logic to define the phallus as a function and he makes clear that this logical function finds its limit with the postulate that there is one element that contravenes the function: the paternal signifier (which Lacan denotes as: $\exists x \, \overline{\Phi x}$).

The logic shifts from identification with the father to identification with the Other, to the assertion "there is one." The father becomes the function of the one that exists, but only as a signifier, opening onto the logic of the not-all; there is one which is not all submitted to the phallic function; castration does not dominate everything, says Lacan in ... *or Worse*. The Other becomes reduced to the Other sex, the one for which a signifier is lacking, i.e. the Other is reduced to its own lack S($\not{A}$).

$$
\begin{array}{cc|cc}
\exists x & \overline{\Phi x} & \overline{\exists x} & \overline{\Phi x} \\
\forall x & \Phi x & \overline{\forall x} & \Phi x \\
\hline
& & \multicolumn{2}{l}{S(\not{A})} \\
\$ & & & \\
& & a & \text{Woman} \\
\Phi & & &
\end{array}
$$

The formulae of sexuation delineate a fundamental dissymmetry between the masculine and the feminine positions, which are but logical positions, so that men and women can put themselves on either side (or both sides) of the chart. Besides, there is no logical relation between the two sides of the chart. In terms of jouissance, Lacan writes, on the feminine side there is the division between phallic jouissance and feminine jouissance, and on the masculine side there is the division between love and jouissance. On the one hand, there is the phallic jouissance as the jouissance of the organ (the phallus is placed on the man's side); on the other hand, he writes $\$ \rightarrow a$ where a is placed on the side of the woman as "the object that puts itself in the place of what cannot be glimpsed of the Other," in the place of the "missing partner" (S20: 63). It should be noted that both men and women, insofar as this is a matter of logical position, are concerned with both sides of the chart. However, the dissymmetry of the chart interprets the inexistence of the sexual relation. It also points out the supplementing/compensating function of love, as an arrow between $\$$ and a which crosses the frontier between men and women.

Love and Transference in the Last Lacan

Now let us follow Lacan's path in *Encore*. Opposing the Platonic conception of love as making one, Lacan tells "a little tale," that of the parakeet that was in love with Picasso:

How could one tell? From the way the parakeet nibbled the collar of his shirt and the flaps of his jacket. Indeed, the parakeet was in love with what is essential to man, namely, his attire [*accoutrement*]. The parakeet was like Descartes, to whom men were only clothes [*habits*] ... walking about [*en pro-ménade*]. Clothes promise debauchery [*ça promet la ménade*] when one takes them off. But this is only a myth [...]. To enjoy a body [*jouir d'un corps*] when there are no more clothes leaves intact the question of what makes the One, that is the question of identification. The parakeet identified with Picasso clothed [*habillé*] (S20: 6).

Lacan points out the narcissistic dimension of love, following Freud, for whom love was addressed to the image of the self, i(*a*), but he points out that beyond the imaginary guise lies the object *a* (the foundation of identification of the One). The promise of the *ménade*, of reaching being, of completeness, is a myth; jouissance can only miss its object. Imaginary identification leaves intact the foundation of identification between *a* and S_1.

The same goes for everything involving love. The habit loves the monk, as they are but one thereby. In other words, what lies under the habit, what we call the body, is perhaps but the remainder [*reste*] I call object *a*.

What holds the image together is a remainder. Analysis demonstrates that love, in its essence, is narcissistic, and reveals that the substance of what is supposedly object-like [*objectal*] – what a bunch of bull – is in fact that which constitutes a remainder in desire, namely, its cause, and sustains desire through lack of satisfaction [*insatisfaction*], and even its impossibility.

Love is impotent, though mutual because it is not aware that it is but the desire to be One, which leads us to the impossibility of establishing the relation between "them-two" [*la relation d'eux*]. The relation between them-two what? – them-two sexes (S20: 6).

Lacan shifts from the ideal of the lost part, and a conception of love as relation and reunion with its complement, to the idea that love, aiming at being, aims at being One; it concerns identification, not being two. "We are but one," he concludes, in the unary sense; one all alone. There is not such a thing as being but only the signifier of the One, and the object *a*, as the foundation of identity. This is what love is concerned with.

Love is thereby closely linked to the inexistence of the sexual relation. There is no sexual relation, but there is love, and "that makes up for the sexual relation."

In the same movement, the object becomes a semblance. If "we never have anything by way of being [*de l'être*] [...] it is in relation to the para-being (*paraître, pare-être*) that we must articulate what makes up for the sexual relation qua non-existent," (S20: 44) says Lacan.

Lacan explains in this seminar that it is in his partner that the subject is looking for the semblance of being that is supposed of the object *a*. "Doesn't the extreme of love, true love, reside in the approach to being?" (S20: 146) asks Lacan. Thus, love aims at an object that is a "substitute for the Other," and on which jouissance depends, which causes it.

> As opposed to what Freud maintains, it is man – I mean he who happens to be male without knowing what to do with it, all the while being a speaking being – who approaches woman, or who can believe that he approaches her [...]. But what he approaches is the cause of his desire that I have designated as object *a*. That is the act of love (S20: 77).

The French word for "approaching" is "*aborder*" and I believe it is not here by chance because Lacan precisely underlines that love is the constitution of an edge (a border) between $ (the $ which he relates earlier to the S$_1$) and *a*. Later on, he says: "On the side of man I have inscribed $ [...] and the Φ that props him up as signifier and is also incarnated in S$_1$," pointing out that "this $ never deals with anything by way of a partner but object *a* inscribed on the other side of the bar" (S20: 80). It is the reason why Lacan can claim that "what makes up for the sexual rapport is, quite precisely, love. He points again to the dimension of love as a letter when he makes clear that love links the One to the Other by the intermediary of the object *a*. It links S_1 to *a*, which is also the function of the letter. It thus writes a relation. The edging function of the letter is relative to the dimension of the object *a* as semblance, as he will also make clear in this seminar. The object *a* stands between the symbolic and the real insofar as it is something cut from the real, a piece of real, a scrap of real, as Jacques-Alain Miller puts it after Lacan (*un bout de réel*). This is what enables the object *a* to be conjoined with the S_1. With love it "stops not being written," or, more precisely, as Lacan puts it, love is what displaces the negation from the "stops not being written" to the "doesn't stop being written" – "doesn't stop, won't stop" (S20: 144) – an echo of the beginning of the seminar where he claims "love demands love. It never stops demanding it. It demands it … *encore*" (S20: 4), pointing to the insatiable, unsatisfactory nature of love, which is always to be written again. Lacan does not adopt any idealistic point of view.

With the displacement of the subject from $barred{S}$ to S_1, from the subject between signifiers to the subject considered as the connection of the master signifier with his jouissance, love becomes even more closely linked to the effect of language, and to transference. Lacan also shifts the stress from meaning to the letter, calling for another type of interpretation based on reading:

What is it we must read therein? Nothing but the effects of those instances of saying [*dires*]. We see in what sense these effects agitate, stir things up, and bother speaking beings. Of course, for that to lead to something it must serve them, and does serve them, by God, in working things out, accommodating themselves, and managing all the same – in a bumbling, stumbling sort of way – to give a shadow of life to the feeling known as love (S20: 46).

Love is linked to the effects of saying, as they give life to love, i.e. to the extraction of the object *a* that commands love, and that gives it life. The analytic experience consists in reading these effects, notably unveiling the function of the object, the roots of one's jouissance, beyond meaning. It is done by detaching the S_1s connected to the subject's jouissance. Lacan adds: "It is insofar as something brutal is played out in writing [*l'écrit*] – namely, the taking as ones of as many ones as we like – that the impasses that are revealed thereby are, by themselves, a possible means of access to being for us and a possible reduction of the function of that being in love" (S20: 49). Analytic experience proceeds from writing, from isolating the one as such (i.e. absolute singularity – the taking as ones of as many ones as we like – but also detaching the S_1s that bear this singularity, that are its mark). This provides the access to object *a*, the possible reduction of the function of being in love. Analytic experience is equated with that of love, in that it aims, like love, at finding an access towards *a* by relying on S_1. We understand again the link of love with the sign. "In love," says Lacan, "what is aimed at is the subject, the subject as such insofar as he is presumed in an articulated sentence," that is to say the One – the S_1. He goes on: "A subject, as such, doesn't have much to do with jouissance. But, on the other hand, his sign is capable of arousing desire. [...] love and sexual jouissance meet up at one point" (S20: 50). Love aims at grasping the object *a* within the other, at being one, but love involves the One and the object through which it is "aroused" by the sign of love. It thus becomes the paradigm of the use of language in psychoanalytical experience.

Lacan thus equates transference and love. He states that the sentence "There is such a thing as One" is to be understood in the sense that there is One all alone:

> We can grasp thereby the crux of what we must clearly call by the name by which the thing resounds throughout the centuries, namely love.
>
> In analysis, we deal with nothing but that, and analysis doesn't operate by any other pathway [that of love and the One all alone]. It is a singular pathway in that it alone allowed us to isolate what I [...] felt I needed to base transference on, insofar as it is not distinguished from love, that is, on the formulation of the "subject supposed to know" (S20: 67).

This implies a twist regarding the notion of knowledge. Lacan explains: "I love the person I assume to have knowledge." He underlines the proximity of love and hatred, reminding us of his own hesitation as to what was involved: love or hatred, as described in Philippe Lacoue Labarthe and Jean-Luc Nancy's reading of Lacan's *Le titre de la lettre*. "Not to know hatred in the least is not to know love in any way either" (S20: 89), he says again later. They proceed to a "desupposition" of his knowledge.

> If I said that they hate me it is because they 'desuppose' that I have knowledge. And why not? Why not if it turns out that that must be the condition for what I call reading? After all, what can I presume Aristotle knew? Perhaps the less I assume he has knowledge, the better I read him (S20: 67).

He later remarks that it is no accident that Freud arms himself with Empedocles' statement that God must be the most ignorant of all beings since he does not know hatred, and adds that if we must overhaul the function of knowledge, it is perhaps because hatred has never been in its proper place. If transference and love are based on the supposition of knowledge, then analytic experience – reading – aims at a desupposition; it works because there is a desupposition at play. The subject can then start reading for himself, but also read beyond meaning. "What is offered to us to be read by that aspect of language that exists, namely, what is woven as an effect of its erosion – that is how I define what is written thereof – cannot be ignored," Lacan adds. Analytic experience puts into play the incompleteness of the Other, its inexistence. The Other is reduced to the Other sex, hence again the link between transference and love. It grasps the cause in what escapes the supremacy of the Other, in the object *a*, and opens a vista onto the inexistence of the sexual relation as the consequence of the fact that there is such thing as the One, but the Other does not exist. Thus, Lacan incites us "to exorcise the good old God," claiming that the Other exists, but as the Other sex, and pointing out that what man approaches "is the cause of his desire that I have designated as *a*. That is the act of love." Transference and love are brought close again.

Love and transference then appear as paths towards truth: that of the object.

As he explains that his aim is to dissociate *a* and A, Lacan notes that love is far from science and yet so close, because it has to do with the letter, i.e. a certain use of the symbolic that borders on the real, as is the case with mathematical letters. He plays on the ambiguity of the word "letter," reminding us that lovers write letters. He remarks, in the same way, that "people have done nothing but speak of love in the analytical discourse," bringing love and transference close together again. He notes: "It is from that alone that psychoanalysis emerged, namely, the objectivisation of the fact that the speaking being still spends time speaking to no avail" (S20: 86), which is also what distinguishes psychoanalysis from science; the aim is close but the means radically differ. He adds, "to speak of love is in itself a jouissance [...] the tangible effect that saying whatever comes to mind [...] is what leads to the *Lustprinzip*, what leads to it directly," he explains. "The *Lustprinzip* is, in effect, based only on the coalescence of *a* with $S(\cancel{A})$" (S20: 84). To speak of love, as we do in analytical practice, is saying what comes to your mind; it is to liberate the control over articulation. It is a way towards the object *a*, as this speech-practice involves jouissance. If speaking of love is not serious, Lacan notes however that "the only thing that one can write that is a bit serious" is a love letter. The love letter is written not only by putting one's pen to paper, but by speaking of love, which aims not at producing meaning but articulates words to jouissance.

He makes this even more precise when he explains that "in the analytic discourse, *a* is supported by S_2, by knowledge, insofar as it is in the place of truth" (S20: 91). He thus provides a commentary on the discourse of the analyst in which *a* addresses $\$$ and produces S_1. In the place of truth, under the first bar, lies S_2. Lacan explains that S_2 supports the truth, that is *a*. The S_1s of the subject, the product of this discourse, are the signifiers that bear the subject's truth, insofar as they are connected to his jouissance.

He underlines the link between truth and jouissance: to demand the whole truth, in legal testimony, is the basis upon which one can judge the convict's jouissance. The analytic cure relies on the same process, except that the horizon of the analytic discourse involves the premise that the whole truth is what cannot be told. The object *a* is a semblance, a semblance of being, a condensation of jouissance in an object produced by symbolic cutting (it is set between the symbolic and the real). Thus Lacan states that "jouissance is questioned (*s'interpelle*), evoked, tracked, and elaborated only on the basis of a semblance," reminding us that "Love itself [...] is addressed to the semblance" and adding "and if it is true that the Other is only reached if it attaches itself (*qu'à s'accoler*) to *a*, the cause of desire, then love is also addressed to the semblance of being. That there-being is not nothing. It is attributed to (*supposé à*) that object that is *a*" (S20: 92). The supposition to know is thereby linked to the supposition of being attached to the object.

Lacan underlines again the inexistence of the Other, reduced to the Other sex, hence the remark that "the Other is only reached through *a*," a semblance of being. Lacan's question at that point makes precise the issue of the supposition of knowledge when the Other does not exist. "The hitch is that the Other, the locus, knows nothing," he points out. The Other becomes reduced to his lack, S(A̶), to the locus of ignorance, to which he adds: "one can no longer hate God if he himself knows nothing." The Other is reduced to the signifier that lacks for Woman, for the Other sex. That is how we can understand this convoluted sentence: "The subjects know, they know [which he opposes to the Other knows]. But all the same, they don't know everything. At this level of the not-everything [*pas-tout*], only the Other doesn't know. It is the Other who constitutes the not-everything, precisely in that the Other is the part of the not-at-all-knowledgeable in the not-everything" (S20: 98). The Other has become the not-all.

This is why love is that through which we have access, through the analytical experience, to the Other, through *a*, through a mere semblance, but also to the not-all, the incompleteness and inexistence of the Other, thereby of the inexistence of the sexual relation. "There is a hole there and that hole is called the Other. It, the Other qua locus in which speech [...] founds truth and, with it, the pact that makes up for the non-existence of the sexual relation," insofar as the lack of a signifier for Woman is the cause of the inexistence of the sexual relation.

The supposition of knowledge leads to desupposition, to have a grasp on the hole called the Other. That is why Lacan can also add: "Love has nothing to do with knowledge," but rather with ignorance, "the passion of being."

Lacan concludes: "I spoke a bit of love. Yet the crux of, or the key to, what I put forward this year concerns the status of knowledge, and I stressed that the use of knowledge could only imply [*représenter*] a jouissance." He adds, "Knowledge is an enigma. That enigma is presented to us by the unconscious, as it is revealed by the analytic discourse. That enigma is enunciated as follows: for the speaking being, knowledge is that which is articulated." He explains that what is articulated is centred on being, but "nothing is' [*rien n'est*], if not insofar as it is said that it is." Articulated language is based upon a void, a lack of being; it does not represent anything but points towards the object as semblance of being around which language revolves and is centred.

Transference, through the analogy with love, thus becomes the analytic experience itself. Lacan adds:

> If I have enunciated that the subject supposed to know is what motivates transference, that is but a particular, specific application of what we find in our experience. I'll ask you to look at the text of what I enunciated here, in the middle of this year, regarding the choice of love. I spoke, ultimately, of recognition, recognition – via signs that are always punctuated enigmatically – of the way in which being is affected qua subject of unconscious knowledge (S20: 144).

Love is a practise of signs; it puts enigma into play rather than meaning. With the object of love in view, its signs revolve around the hole of the Other and the object *a*, implying jouissance more than representing anything.

The analytic experience, like love, or rather *as* love, opens onto the inexistent sexual relation:

> There is no such thing as sexual relationship because one's jouissance of the Other taken as a body is always inadequate – perverse, on the one

hand, insofar as the Other [to be understood as the Other sex] is reduced to object *a*, and crazy and enigmatic, on the other, I would say (*ibid*).

Love and transference bring us to the brink of the subject's unconscious knowledge; the knowledge that there is only the hole of the Other, and jouissance. Lacan adds:

> Isn't it on the basis of the confrontation with this impasse, with the impossibility by which a real is defined, that love is put to the test? Regarding one's partner, love can only actualise what, in a sort of poetic flight, in order to make myself understood, I called courage – courage with respect to this fatal destiny. But is it courage that is at stake or pathways of recognition? That recognition is nothing other than the way in which the relationship said to be sexual – that has become a subject-to-subject relationship, the subject being the effect of unconscious knowledge – stops not being written (*ibid*).

Love is also what makes up for the sexual relation, and what makes the subject's unconscious knowledge stop not being written, through recognition. Love creates a link between $, S$_1$ and *a* by tending towards *a*, reaching beyond meaning, towards jouissance (this is what Lacan calls recognition, the recognition of the hole of the Other that can lead beyond what does not cease not to be written). The subject-to-subject relation is that which writes the connection; it stops not being written.

> All love, subsisting only on the basis of the "stops not being written," tends to make the negation shift to the "doesn't stop being written, doesn't stop, won't stop [*ne cesse pas de s'écrire*]. Such is the substitute that – by the path of existence, not of the sexual relationship, but of the unconscious, which differs therefrom – constitutes the destiny as well as the drama of love (S20: 145).

In other words, since there is no sexual relation, love, as a suppletion [*suppléance*], can but keep on trying to write, again and again, an ephemeral link. Love approaches being as such in the encounter, just as in analytic experience, but it is also in this approach "that something emerges that makes being into what is only sustained by the fact of missing each other [*se rater*]." Subjects have a relation to *a*, and not to each other as a complementary part that would provide a supplement of being. "Doesn't the extreme of love, true love, reside in the approach to being? And true love [...] gives way to hatred," concludes Lacan, in the sense that the only being there is (and which *is* not) is *a*. Love opens on the desupposition of knowledge, the lack of being, a grasp on the object, and the destiny of missing it always, as the object is lost; it is only a semblance, a semblance of being. The effect of love, says Lacan, is "to throw into question the existence of the soul (being)" (S20: 84).

Centring the analytic experience upon transference, Lacan equates it with that of love. He will later modulate that equivalence in the sense that love is considered on the level of "writing a letter," whereas the cure rather consists in "reading that letter."

And Further On…

In his *Seminar XXI, Les Non-dupes errent*, Lacan reminds us that truth is an effect of analytic experience. He evokes an "odour of truth" like the *odore di femina* of Mozart's Don Juan. It is an effect of speech. He adds that transference is not a means but the effect of analytic experience. It is a result, insofar as speech reveals something that has nothing to do with it, it is the knowledge that exists within language. In other words, speaking reveals truth, which can only be said between words; it reveals the dimension of the real, of the object. Language is the medium of analytic experience – it puts transference into play – because language causes jouissance, which is at stake through speech. Saying [*le dire*] reveals the object. Jouissance is at stake while speaking, but mostly, with the concept of saying, Lacan accentuates the dimension of enunciation, of the function of the S_1, connected with jouissance. In the same extract, Lacan remarks that language is not knowledge but that it proceeds from the S_1. We may add, then, that it puts object *a* into play, as the remainder of the mark of language, of the action of the S_1.

Transference is an effect of speech, of saying. Lacan adds: "Does it mean that transference gives access to truth? It gives access to something that constitutes truth, but the truth which only transference reveals, it reveals the truth of Love."[8] Transference is no longer equated with love, but it is the means by which its truth is revealed, i.e. the something that constitutes truth, the object *a*, and, as a result, the inexistence of the sexual relation. Lacan provides a new version of the supposition of knowledge in the analytic experience by unveiling the assemblage between the real, the symbolic and the imaginary – the interaction of saying, language, and jouissance.

He explains that the affinities of transference with the revelation of the truth of love are why transference is "expelled." He evokes the post-Freudian "liquidation of transference"; transference is what has to be evacuated insofar as it reveals a truth rejected by the post-Freudians. He opposes to this the Lacanian issue which consists of accepting to be the dupe of the unconscious, not loving the unpleasant knowledge of the unconscious, but accepting that there is the real that drives us, at the root of a disharmonic unconscious of which we cannot but be the dupe.

This means, as he later develops in *Seminar XXIV, L'insu que sait de l'une bévue s'aile à mourre*, accepting that there is no Other and, therefore, that there is no one that knows; the subject is the one who speaks and hears, and he is irremediably divided between speaking and hearing [*entendre*].[9] The only knowledge that there is is that of the unconscious, of the effects of the signifier. The end of analysis implies the separation of the subject from the Other and also from himself. He reaches the point where he has to admit that there is but One, not the Other. There is One, but nothing else. The One dialogues alone, he is the one who knows, not the one supposed to know. What remains unknown of the unconscious is love: *"l'insu que sait de l'une-bevue,"* as Lacan translates *Bewusst*, the unconscious, *"S'aile à [c'est la] mourre."* The sentence also lets us hear *"insuccès"* – unsuccess of the unconscious. It places the unconscious on the side of equivocation, on the side of the S_1. Lacan finally plays on the homophony with *"mourre,"* a game of chance between two partners, pointing towards the inexistence of the sexual relation. The unconscious is brought back again to the real, in its two aspects, the object, the scrap of jouissance, and the non-rapport. Transference dissolves at the point where it has opened onto the certainty of the real, onto what stops being written and what cannot stop not being written.

The outcome is "a new love" for the unconscious, but also for one's partner, since taking into account the true nature of love, the inexistence of the sexual relation, helps us to live love in an easier way.

Lecture given in English at the London Society of the NLS, 19 May 2018

The Littoral Condition: A Reading of "Lituraterre"

Sophie Marret-Maleval

The Littoral Condition:
A Reading of "Lituraterre"

Sophie Marret-Maleval

In spite of its difficulty, "Lituraterre" is an essential text of Lacan's teaching.[1] It constitutes one of the major steps at the turning point of the 1970s from where Lacan lays the foundation for his later teaching. He specifies in it the concept of the "letter," which had been present since the beginning of his teachings, and gives it a more essential scope. "Lituraterre" marks a new distancing from the register of truth, in which the letter as specified in "The Instance of the Letter..."[2] remains the vehicle, even though reduced to the signifier of the truth of desire, the phallus. The letter becomes correlated with the register of jouissance. This text already participates in what Jacques-Alain Miller refers to as the sixth paradigm of jouissance, that of the non-rapport, through which "Lacan truly cuts the branch on which all his teaching was sitting."[3] He points out that where language and structure have a function of "the capture of the living organism," the non-relation appears as the limit of the structure's hold. Speech is no longer conceived as communication but as jouissance. The articulation S_1–S_2, meaning, becomes secondary with respect to S_1a, the mark of the signifier on the body which has the effect of jouissance, a movement which clearly informs "Lituraterre."

Jacques-Alain Miller notes that this paradigm pushes "the concept of language, the earlier concept of speech as communication, as well as the concepts of the big Other, the Name of the Father, and the phallic symbol [...] to the point of collapse into semblants" (PN34: 64-5). Which is to say that they are no longer primary and structural, but derived fictions. These terms are reduced to "a function of stapling together elements that are fundamentally disconnected."

The text was written during *Seminar XVIII: D'un discours qui ne serait pas du semblant*, of which it constitutes the seventh chapter. It was subsequently published as the introduction to an issue of the journal *Littérature* in 1971.

Littering the Letter

Lacan "legitimises" the title of his text through a reference to the *Dictionnaire Étymologique de la Langue Latine: Histoire des Mots* by Ernout and Meillet, returning to the Latin root, *lino*, of the word *litura*, which signifies erasure. He also inscribes in it a reference to Joyce, as much for its neological character as for its equivocation, recalling the wordplay of "a letter, a litter," which, by the substitution of a letter, associates the letter with the rubbish. It should be noted that this is probably a borrowing of Joyce from Lewis Carroll, who writes literature with two t's – *litterature* – making apparent the word "litter" in literature – that which is literature's debt to litter.[4]

Let's note that Lacan emphasises the inventive character of his title by evoking *"contrepet"* or "spoonerism," the "inversion" to the ear, a term that situates again what his approach is about (Lacan's words are always carefully chosen) when he starts from equivocation as the foundation of the formations of the unconscious; and to which he will give a new turn when it is no longer a question of using it to lead down the path to repressed truth but to jouissance.

He had thus followed in the footsteps of Joyce, five years before *The Sinthome* (the seminar of 1975-6), where he emphasises that he is going "straight [...] to the best of what can be expected from psychoanalysis at its end" (HB9: 29), whether by making "litter of the letter," or by using the letter to cradle jouissance. It is the aim of psychoanalysis that he redefines through the same movement. Lacan asks if it is the *sicut palea* of Saint Thomas Aquinas that returns to Joyce (we know that Aquinas is a major reference for Joyce). Jacques-Alain Miller specifies that "these two Latin words mean 'like dung' and would have been the answer of Saint Thomas Aquinas at the end of his life when he was asked what his work, his *Summa Theologica*, meant to him."[5] What must be understood is that his work is not worth much, and that there will be nothing left; some translations even evoke the comparison of his work to straw. Rather,

Lacan emphasises that Joyce's knowledge lies in his denunciation of the emptiness of meaning, his intuition about how to get along with the letter and the manure of which it is a part.

Psychoanalysis must go down the same path and reveal where language and jouissance are joined. Lacan points out a convergence between the movement of contemporary literature, of which Joyce is a part, and the movement of psychoanalysis, which he then refers to as "the slackening of the ancient bond," i.e. the end of the myth as a historical fact.

The change of epistemological paradigm and the inexistence of the Other paved the way for a new path for literature and culture, thus sounding the death knell for myth. Let us recall that Lacan in the previous seminar evoked myth in connection with the *mi-dire*, or half-saying, of truth, the sister of jouissance; here, with the letter, he takes a step further, beyond myth and truth. Jouissance is no longer to be glimpsed between the lines, between the signifiers, as an impossible to say, but the letter staples and collects jouissance, it is read from the S_1. In *Encore*, Lacan will call it another reading, different from the practice of deciphering meaning.

In "Lituraterre," Lacan points out that it is by using this knowledge that contemporary literature moves ahead, it no longer rests on myths, or on meaning. He pays tribute to Beckett, who "balances" the rise of the imperative of the superego as an imperative of jouissance: "the debit that forms the refuse of our being." He reveals it because of his knowledge of the inexistence of the Other, of God, through "confession," that is to say the renewal of the object *a* as a remainder, and by "having it," the object *a* which he puts to work by manipulating what lies outside meaning, the equivoque. Like Beckett, Lacan is responsible for revealing the other side of civilisation; psychoanalysis opens onto the path of the treatment of jouissance by the letter.

A Change of Configuration

Subsequently he situates "Lituraterre" in the context of a "change of configuration" with regard to writing in the field of literary studies. It differs from the vision carried by the textbooks of literature, for which the written tradition would have resulted from the oral tradition, that of "song, spoken myth, and dramatic processions" (HB9: 30) and of which it would have been a "rehashing of leftovers." If literature is a rehashing of leftovers, it is not in the sense of a "collocation in written form" of the oral tradition which would fix it, contributing to its readability and meaning. Opposing this communal vision, Lacan asserts that the letter enters into an intimate rapport with jouissance, that it proceeds towards the recovery of a certain object by way of sublimation, as he had already indicated in his homage to Lewis Carroll,[6] or even that it celebrates "the silent wedding of the empty life and the indescribable object," as he says at the conclusion of his homage to Marguerite Duras.[7] Lacan moves ahead more precisely in "Lituraterre," with the letter knotting empty life and the indescribable object; it is located at the joint of the object and the signifier, it treats jouissance.

Lacan notes the inadequacy of the Oedipal orientation for finding one's bearings in contemporary literature, pointing out that literary criticism did not receive any impetus from psychoanalysis when it was based on an Oedipal interpretation. He targets Marie Bonaparte, whom he cites later with regard to Edgar Allan Poe,[8] but, surprisingly, he evokes Freud's text on Dostoevsky, which is undoubtedly the most psychobiographical of his essays concerning literature, in order to mark a rupture, a turning point, not only in the way in which psychoanalysis must approach the work of art, but also in the way in which it must advance beyond the Oedipus in order to learn something from contemporary artists, as he himself will do with Joyce.

Lacan notes that "Lituraterre" takes place in the context of a "change of configuration that boasts a slogan promoting the written." He follows in the footsteps of contemporary philosophers and literary critics like Barthes, Derrida, Bakhtin. This context shows "a shift of interests which suits me better," he emphasises, in the sense that literary studies after Roland Barthes have emphasised the literality of the narrative (and no longer a truth, biographical or historical in particular, which is external to the text and which allows us to account for its meaning). When he mentions the fact that "it is only today that Rabelais is finally being read," he is referring to Mikhail Bakhtin, a Russian literary critic whose thesis on Rabelais caused a scandal in the USSR in 1946 and had to wait until 1965 to be published. His theory of carnivalesque writing[9] and dialogism[10] had an important influence on the French post-structuralists, in particular Julia Kristeva, with her concept of intertextuality. Lacan nonetheless adopts a very critical stance towards Jacques Derrida, who he directly targets through the reference to the "slogan for the promotion of the written word," denouncing his concept of the trace and the primacy of the written word.

Lacan is keen to set psychoanalysis apart from literary criticism, denouncing "the psychoanalyst lacking inventiveness" who would incautiously venture into this field, evoking "the unevenness of his practice in motivating the faintest literary judgement" (HB9: 30). Here he explicitly targets Marie Bonaparte, but also Derrida, who contributed to closely associating psychoanalysis with literature.

He reminds us that he is "less implicated in this as an author than people imagine" in this context of the "promotion of writing," that is, in the structuralist and post-structuralist movement, which began with literature and with which he is often associated, through invoking that his writings are not literary works but composed of "open letters" and "reports which are a function of Congresses" from which his teachings proceed.

Avowal, Elision, and the Hole

Thus, after these remarks aimed at situating his proposal and the ethical orientation of psychoanalysis, he returns to his commentary on Edgar Allan Poe's story, "The Purloined Letter," which he had chosen (against chronology) as the opening text of his *Écrits*. He emphasises that since the beginning of his teachings, he had given particular importance to the letter through his reading of this story. He recalls that the story is based on the trajectory of a letter whose content is unknown and which, as he stated in his seminar, always arrives at its destination and has a feminising effect on the one who holds it. The letter is, then, the phallus carrying the meaning of castration. Thus, Lacan indicates that a distinction must be made more precisely than before between the signifier, which can enter into the game of metaphor, correlated to meaning, and the letter, which conveys the message of castration which lies beyond meaning and excludes all metaphor.

In "Lituraterre," he distinguishes his reading from that of Marie Bonaparte. Poe, he says, forms this message on the letter, which, "by not spelling it out as such," he all the more rigorously reveals. As with the reference to Beckett, Lacan links the practice of the letter to avowal, that is to say, to an unveiling that does not pass through meaning but rather through elision (elision of meaning but also of the phallus, the bearer of castration at the least, whose function operates without the knowledge of the protagonists and the reader). He reproaches Marie Bonaparte for having rather sought to block the elucidation of this elision, of the function of the phallus and the letter, by turning it into a psychobiography.

He then moves on to Derrida, reproaching him for reading him badly, evoking "Le facteur de la vérité,"[11] where he hadn't grasped why Lacan says that a letter *always* arrives at its destination because it bears castration, nor why he proposes "to psychoanalysis the letter as pending," indicating that this last term is to be understood as showing the failure of the letter, that is to say its lack of representation, its lack of meaning. It "forms a *hole*" in the Enlightenment [*lumières*], he notes. There wasn't any "hermeneutic semantics," therefore, and Derrida did not understand that Lacan was, on the contrary, aiming at this hole in meaning. This fundamental point is also the one that separates Lacan from the philosopher for whom the letter symbolises writing, that is to say, content, whereas for Lacan it traces a void at the heart of the signifier. For Derrida the letter remains the representation of writing, whereas for Lacan it is the failure of all representation.

To grasp this notion of hole, which he brings in opposition to the Enlightenment, to Reason, to truth, and to meaning, Lacan evokes optics and the photon, which is to say a conception of vision based on a hole in the visible. For Lacan it is a question of a new approach to the hole, in relation to the "Seminar on *The Purloined Letter*," pointing towards the object and no longer simply related to the phallus as a signifier of castration, of want-of-being, and of desire.

Literature, at its source, is based less on a "psychobiographical idea" of repression (cf. Marie

Bonaparte), and it is up to psychoanalysis to grasp this in order to learn from it. Knowledge is on the side of literary texts, but it is conveyed by the letter, that is to say, without anyone's knowing. In return, it is psychoanalysis that knows "the enigma on its side," which elaborates the hole in knowledge in order to build its foundations, that which can allow a renewal of literary criticism. That discipline will only be able to renew itself when "psychoanalysis is there so that the texts can pit themselves against it," (HB9: 31) which is to say that they may be deciphered in the light of the enigma that only psychoanalysis can unveil. It is the enigma that is the very object of psychoanalysis, and only psychoanalysis makes it operative.

Targeting Marie Bonaparte, he extends his criticism to the post-Freudians, who are too captive to truth and knowledge. He says of them that they are "exercised by psychoanalysis," "rather than practising it," "taken as a body," and points out that if they don't understand the real, the object, they are just a plaything. Would it be going too far to notice this mention of the body, which already shifts the unconscious towards the *parlêtre* of the later teachings, approaching the *"en corps"* of *Encore*?

As for knowledge, he specifies that knowledge *"en échec*, in check, [...] is not a failure of knowledge," but rather invites analysts to produce knowledge on the limits of knowledge, on the object, and not to conclude that it is enough to stick to a position of debility, while stigmatising at the same time any atheoretical position beyond the post-Freudians.

Recalling that he made the letter the "reason behind the unconscious" in "The Instance of the Letter," Lacan indicates that this is a false rhetorical question, that it is not a question of the letter remaining a dead letter. It is a question of reminding psychoanalysts that theory is alive (not to take the pretext of the hole in knowledge to know nothing, to sound the death knell for theory, since it is a dead letter) and underlining the need to hear the importance of this new concept. It is also about moving away from the concept of the letter correlated to a want-of-being for the subject of desire and the being-unto-death in order to link the letter to what is alive in jouissance.

Littorals and Frontiers

He situates the letter as that which insists, as the motor of repetition, and which is not "there by rights," that is to say, probably, outside the law of language, outside the Other, dissociated from the articulation S_1–S_2. It is linked to repression, to the drive, but from then on to what is outside the grip of language, to the object. First of all, he mentions "the bifidity to which all measure commits"; that is to say that it presupposes two faces, a real face and a signifying face. And he asks, "Is there nothing in the real that forgoes this mediation?" In other words, he asserts that the real is only grasped from the symbolic but tries to distinguish the letter from the mathematical measure (insufficient to really grasp the letter, it remains linked to judgment, it puts forth a signifying polarity that is unfit to grasp the border between the real and the symbolic, while the real, with the notion of measure, is grasped in and by the signifier). Lacan also dismisses the notion of the frontier, which "by separating two territories, symbolises that they are the same for whosoever crosses it, that they have a common measure." The abstract line of the border symbolically separates two zones that can be similar in nature. For him, the notion of a border is one which seems to him to belong to biology. He takes the example of Von Uexküll, who is interested in the effect of the *Innenwelt* (the inner world) on the *Umwelt* (the world outside a subject inasmuch as it is, for him, an environment), that is, for whom everything is the effect of a frontier. He opposes psychoanalysis to the mathematical model and to that of biology. It must equip itself with its own tools that allow it to take into account the radical heterogeneity of the symbolic and the real and the notion of an edge between these two dimensions. It is the notion of "littoral" that can take us down these other paths, rather than those of the border or that of measurement or the signification of the real.

The letter is littoral, Lacan asserts – it is what makes the border between the symbolic and the real, between knowledge and jouissance. The littoral is the line that marks the edge between land and sea. The littoral character of the letter comes to mark the heterogeneity of the territories that it separates in contrast to a frontier that symbolises the "common measure." The letter of "Lituraterre" is no longer that of "The Instance of the Letter…". Indeed, in *Seminar XVIII*, as Leander Pasqual shows in his thesis, "the phallus is no longer considered as the signifier of desire, that is to say, as the signifier of the dialectic of being and having, which is written (-φ)."[12] It "becomes the name of that which is not articulated either in speech or in desire, namely jouissance itself. The latter is referred to here as the forbidden, which is written (Φ)." From the quilting point between the symbolic and the imaginary in "The Signification of the Phallus," it becomes a quilting point between the symbolic and the real. The question of the littorality of the letter seems to be well correlated with this shift, but, as Leander Pasqual points out, it is with the phallus becoming a pure semblant. Jacques-Alain Miller points out that "Lacan specialises the term 'semblant' for what falls between the symbolic and the real. That is to say, he specialises it for what is definitively of the order of the signifier, for what comes from the symbolic but precisely which does not hold up upon approaching the real."[13] From then on, like the clouds of Lacan's apologia, the phallus is doomed to give way, says Leander Pasqual. Indeed, Lacan will then specify that the letter is what precipitates the rupture of the semblant. It is "the writing in the real of what arises from the semblant." It "is as much at the service of knowledge as it is at the service of jouissance."

To define this concept, Lacan situates the letter precisely away from the phallus, which for its part is symbolic. It should rather be defined on the basis of the S_1 and the object a.

$S_1 a$

The S_1, in fact, translates, in the same way as the phallus, the elision of the subject, between signifiers, deducible from the second signifier. Whereas the phallus emphasises the subject as want-of-being, the S_1 accentuates the identification by the unary trait, and comes to the gaze of the S_2. It is the S_1–S_2 link that Lacan attacks here when he shifts the emphasis to the outside-meaning and the object, in a movement where the question of alienation, of the bond between the subject and the Other, gives way to that of separation and the bond between the subject and the object, as Éric Laurent indicates. This displacement occurs when the Other loses its eminence, when the object is the Other of the subject.

Éric Laurent shows us that the subject is no longer represented only as want-of-being, either by the phallus or by the object: "The subject, when he cannot be represented, when he is no longer represented in the Other, when the Other is no longer that place where he is alienated, where he inscribes himself, but becomes the desert of *l'Achose* [*th'Athing*], then the subject instead clings to what is its mooring point, the object *a* and the letter, Lacan tells us, and becomes littoral."[14] The object is lodged in the hole of the Other, a One more [*Un en plus*], to which the subject clings like a child to its teddy bear,[15] when the Other leaves it. The identification through the S_1 then arrives in relation to the identification with the object.

The letter draws the edge of the hole in knowledge, says Lacan in "Lituraterre". Knowledge is made up of the articulation S_1–S_2, or, more precisely, S_2 shapes knowledge. The edge of the hole in knowledge is approached by the S_1, an asemantic signifier that represents the subject as One, as unary, and names the object of its jouissance. He notes that the letter "invokes," in this hole, the jouissance that fills it.

We can hear that the letter (like that which breaks apart from the semblant, which undoes itself) con-vokes, calls on, jouissance (the signifier becomes the cause of jouissance) in the place of God, hence the reference to invocation. The Father is reduced to the hole in the Other in which the object *a* is lodged, or even to the object itself. The letter is broken down into a signifying face and a real face: S_1 (signifying face) makes a hole in knowledge; *a* (real face) fills it. The letter is formed by the couple $S_1 a$. The Father gets divided between the One (who will go on to give the paternal exception in the formulae of sexuation) and the Other, related here to the object (as the Other of the subject), but also to its lack, announcing in *Encore* its reduction to the Other sex, to $S(\bar{A})$.[16]

It remains to be seen how the unconscious, which is "effect of language," "commands this function of the letter" (HB9: 32), Lacan notes. He recalls that he has identified the unconscious, until then, in strictly signifying terms. It is structured like a lan-guage and the subject is what one signifier represents for another signifier. The letter of the unconscious, the phallus, was very much about the signifier. In the fifth paradigm, jouissance circulated with the signifiers, between the signifiers, and the interpretation of the unconscious in structural terms remained possible. How then can we conceive of the unconscious with this displacement of the concept of the letter, when the articulation of S_1–S_2 is undone in favour of an identification through jouissance and the unary trait? Lacan indicates that the unconscious "commands" the function of the letter (again anticipating the affirmation that the signifier is the cause of jouissance). The answer that Lacan will bring to this question lies in the rupture of the semblant, that is to say of the articulation S_1–S_2, from whence the letter falls.

It seems to me that a new inversion will take place with his very last teachings. When it is the sinthome, which gets written as $S_1 a$, that is situated in the place of commandment, that is to say the first bite of S_1 on the body that causes the fall of the object, we find that meaning and the articulation S_1–S_2 become secondary.

The Letter, the Impression, and the Trace

When it is the unconscious that commands, according to "Lituraterre," the letter is not primary. Lacan takes advantage of this, once again, to criticise the theses of Derrida, the primacy of the letter which is, for him, the trace to which all writing, all signifying articulation, refers. Lacan contrasts his own conception of the letter with this. It is "the proper instrument for the writing of discourse" (Lacan wrote his four discourses with four letters, making symbolic use of them, like the letters of mathematics, to reduce psychoanalysis to its logic). It is "not improper [...] symbolising certain signifier-effects," he continues, where it is to be understood as participating in the metaphorical or metonymic use of language. "But that the letter be primary within these effects is not a must," as the initial lesson of *Seminar XVIII* indicates in a more developed manner.[17] Éric Laurent comments: "In this way, he challenges the primary place of the bar that divides metaphor and metonymy. He says that this can serve for that, but it is not sufficient. Thus, he criticises himself, as he often does."[18] Éric Laurent specifies that by challenging its function as a primary instrument, Lacan is attacking the Western tradition with regard to writing, while he also rejects the notion of the letter as the primary impression that Derrida uses to define his own conception of the trace. Behind the reference to Derrida and his text "Freud and the Scene of Writing," there is Lacan's departure from Freud's "Mystic Writing-Pad" (SE19), as he specifies more explicitly later. He pays homage, however, to Freud for the paths opened up in the "Project for a Scientific Psychology" (SE1), although his own reading did not lead him to deduce that writing is an impression. Nevertheless, he emphasises that Freud, in his approach to the formations of the unconscious (through substitution, condensation and displacement), has grasped that letters are "signifier-effects." For all that, he distances himself from him again (specifying that this "confusional" discourse could only have arisen from the one that matters to him, that is to say from the discourse of psychoanalysis, from Freud), and probably also from Derrida. The thesis of the latter is a product of the emergence of the discourse of psychoanalysis inside the university discourse, "knowledge put to use on the basis of the semblant." As a consequence, the notion of the trace elaborated by Derrida struggles to escape from the logic of the signifier.

The analytical experience is situated in another discourse, Lacan stresses, it is the only one to grasp the littoral function of the letter. This experience is the one he invests in, that is to say that he organises it and remedies its weaknesses according to the definitions of the Littré dictionary. The experience of the real can only be grasped through analytical discourse. Lacan notes, however, the difficulty of being the one who finds himself transmitting it (it "confesses itself from him," it is necessary for him to venture to the edges of language, of formalisation, in order to do so). We also hear that the renewal of psychoanalysis is produced by its saying, that it requires the act and the enunciation of a subject, the S_1. He notes that he would have preferred to have been spared this, that what matters to him is that he could be bothered. The exclamation "Thank God!" added in this connection is probably not insignificant. It is an ironic reference, marking the reduction of the invocation of God's name to a rhetorical formula. God, the Other, has given way again to the S_1 and the object *a*, which he supports, and which is the cause of his hassles.

From thereon Lacan clarifies the specificity of the letter. He states that "the crux of what seems to me to produce the letter as a consequence, and of language" (HB9: 33) is "that whoever speaks, inhabits it," which leads him on to define the relationship of the letter to the unary trait and jouissance.

The Trip to Japan

Lacan then sets about developing his conception of the letter, explaining how it came to him from a trip to Japan. The notion of travel is intimately linked to the littoral function, whereas the *Umwelt* [environment] makes it impossible: with such a compass it would be a matter of going from the same to the same, it would be tantamount to being content to sing "Partons" [a French song whose title means "let's go"]. How can we understand this reference? It evokes the departure of troops for the war, drawing courage from a patriotic song, that is to say the journey is conceived as a conquest, along with the dimension of illusion that accompanies it; it also evokes Offenbach's *Orpheus in the Underworld* when the gods of Olympus joyfully leave for hell to cheat their boredom, singing "let's go" (a nod, perhaps, to patriotic songs). In both cases it is the dimension of the real, of what happens on the other side of the lines, that is veiled.

In "Lituraterre," Lacan notes that he has taken a new route for the first time, "thumbing his nose at the imprecise routes of Derrida," as Éric Laurent comments (HB9: 62). Lacan goes on to explain that it is an air route that had just opened over the plains of Siberia, but "a desert route, because the Soviets wanted to be sure that no spy plane would photograph their installations." Lacan says that it was no longer "as off-limits as the first time." How can we fail to hear again here the evocation of a new type of crossing in his teaching, a beyond the Oedipus? The littoral is not the barrier of *The Ethics* between the signifier and the Thing that only a few heroes can cross; with the littoral Lacan moves towards a conception of jouissance which is no longer jouissance "forbidden [*interdite*] to whoever speaks."[19] It was not the outward journey, along the Arctic Circle, that "read" to him what he saw in the plains of Siberia. It was his encounter with the Japanese language, in relation to the letter, that enabled him to read it differently. He also points out the contingency according to which his text would not have seen the light of day if the Russians had allowed flying over cities and industrial and military installations. He speaks of an accidental condition, but not wholly so. Indeed, he points to the work of the death drive in civilisation, the "accident of a pile-up of slaughter" – *accident d'un amoncellement de l'occire*, a play on words that links "occident" to the death drive – the accident being the death drive, not as ignored as one might think, since it can be deliberately maintained and masked. Paradoxically, the ban placed on one route frees the second, which reveals the other side of jouissance, linked to the littoral.

What made what he saw on his return legible for him, he says, is that he had grasped, with the Japanese calligraphic letter, the littoral condition. There he encountered a "little bit too much," a "just what it takes for me to feel it," which is perceptible in Japan in the letter, in its art, and which is "what its language is eminently affected with." The question of jouissance in language becomes perceptible to him with the letter in Japan; what affects language is the letter, the correlation of the S_1 and jouissance. This "too much," he notes, "stems from what their art conveys of it." Via calligraphy, painting "demonstrates its marriage to the letter." He says he has been fascinated by the *kakémonos*, hung in museums, bearing inscriptions that make it possible to measure "what is being elided from them in the cursive," (HB9: 34) that is to say, what Western writing veils. It seems to establish two models of writing – an Occidental writing, marked by repression, and an Oriental writing, based on the letter. With the letter, the emphasis is on the singular; with the signifier, on the universal – a characteristic, he notes, which appears to him all the more so as he is a novice, he does not read Chinese, but he takes the opportunity to specify that the important thing is not the meaning, the universal. Calligraphy reveals that the letter is the writing of the unary trait ("the singular quality of the hand"), of the S_1 (the brushstroke, its particularity, is also the painter's signature) and recuperation of jouissance (the *kakémono* is given to be seen, inviting the gaze more than meaning).

Papeludun and Hun-en-Peluce[20]

Lacan describes the singular as "supporting a firmer shape"[21]; I understand this as pointing towards a greater firmness of the conjunction $S_1 a$ than that of conjunction of S_1 and S_2 or structure, which he will indicate later as breakable. The singular of the hand, the brushstroke, adds the dimension of "*papeludun,*" that is to say a unary One, S_1. The letter marks the absolute difference, where there is no two, no S_2. Could we go so far as to decipher in this neologism the word "pope" [*pape*] as associated with the One-all-alone, that is to say the reduction of the father to S_1, the passage from the Other to the One? He introduces here a second neologism: the singular "adds the *demansion* of the *papeludun,*" a portmanteau word which replaces 'di' with 'de'; perhaps it is necessary to hear "*deux*" and "*dit,*" an equivoque on the fact that dimension requires a two-ness precisely when the letter implies the "*papeludun*" or not more than one. We think of the definition of the point whose specificity is not having a dimension; the "*papeludun*" is a torsion, an elimination of the dimension which presupposes the two. There is no "*dit-mension*"; what is excluded from the "*demansion*" is the said, to which comes the "*papeludun,*" the unary trait, the one-all-alone. I also hear the trans-linguistic equivoque "mansion," an English signifier which means home, and "*demansion,*" an equivoque which is reminiscent of the previous "whoever speaks inhabits it,"[22] knotting the letter to the said, to S_1, which constitutes the abode of the one and from which the two takes its departure, wherever it is located.

From the "*papeludun*," from the S_1, there is evoked "what I establish of the subject in the Hun-en-Peluce." Éric Laurent clarified that this is about the object *a*. The subject is established by its being moored to the object when the Other is no longer there. It echoes the equivoque "*Un en Peluche*," the teddy bear to which the child clings when its mother is away. The Hun-en-Peluce makes heard the conjunction of the familiar (*en peluche*) and the strangeness, the barbarity, the Hun, the One to which the warlord Attila is reduced, but also the jouissance outside the law of language, the two dimensions of the subject which is moulded (S_1 and *a*, the *a* being attached to S_1 by the letter). The dimension of beyond-meaning finally springs forth against the clarity of sense, against the bonding of S_1–S_2 (which is the subject of the derision of the cuddly toy, *peluche*; there is no additional "one" and no S_2 since 1+1 would make 2) with the dimension of beyond-meaning carried by the equivoque.

The subject is no longer located between S_1 and S_2 but between S_1 and *a*. The Hun-en-Peluce "furnishes the anxiety of th'Athing." In "Six Paradigms of Jouissance," Jacques-Alain Miller indicates that Lacan, once again, summons the Thing in his very last teaching, against the manageable side of the object; here the Thing has just designated the void, that which accommodates jouissance under the category of object *a*. However, Lacan writes "th'Athing," in a single word, with a capital letter; he reduces the Other to the Thing, or to its emptiness.

In the initial conference, Lacan specified: "It is very useful [Hun-en-Peluce], it is encountered in place of what I call th'Athing [...] and it fills it up with the object *a*."[23] The letter is made of the conjunction of the One and the object *a* which comes in place of the Other, whose functions are divided between One and *a*. It is the conjunction of the unary trait, of One and of *a*, which counters the anxiety of the void of the Other.

The verb "to furnish," which again evokes that which contributes to living in a place, in the sense of taking possession of it, also points to a recovery of jouissance in the letter, which he then specifies: "What I connote with a little *a* here [in the calligraphy] acts as the object by virtue of being the stake in the wager that is won with ink and brush" (HB9: 34). Calligraphy is the writing of the unary trait and the recovery of surplus jouissance; the "little bit too much" correlated with the test of affect, that which moves, that which sets the subject in motion.

Streaming

In this text the writing of the sinthome ($S_1 a$) is sketched out through the release of the littoral function of the letter. Lacan gives, from then on, an illustration of this through what he sees when he flies over Siberia in an aeroplane. Between the clouds, he sees a "streaming of waters" in the plains. The only trace to appear there, the streaming makes a trace, it digs a trace. Lacan responds again to Derrida, with the trace being conjugated with jouissance. The streaming indicates a relief, it operates in this relief as Lacan specifies, it participates in the constitution of the relief, digs the furrow in the Siberian plain. The streaming is the image of the letter as the digging of the furrow under the effect of the water that fills it. It is the object *a* that makes a hole in knowledge, but it is also cut out of the real, "a piece of the real"; a semblant, Lacan would later say, is linked to an edge, the furrow, the S_1.

The only vegetation of the plain is constituted by reflections, which "pushes into the shade that which does not glisten back" (HB9: 34) (streaming). In other words, there is no trace (the reflection) other than that attached to the shimmering produced by the streaming. "The reflection of the runoff operates as a trace that indicates nothing else," notes Leander Pasqual (on p. 211 of his thesis). It is also the reflection attached to the shimmering which creates the shadow, that is to say that the elision (that of the subject) is the result of the letter and not of the pair S_1–S_2, as Lacan will go on to develop.

Lacan, in fact, opposes to the "blotting out of no trace whatsoever that might be from before" (Derrida's theory) the image of the streaming, conjugated with the rupture of the semblant (which is the cloud, the signifier) and which evokes jouissance.

"The streaming is a cluster [*bouquet*] of the first trait and what effaces it" (HB9: 34) affirms Lacan. The term "bouquet" combines the notions of assembly and product (we also think of the final bouquet, the climax of a fireworks display). The letter assembles the S_1 and that which erases the first trait, *a*. It results from the first trait, from the incidence of language at its point of insertion.

The object is understood as that which erases the trace. If we follow the initial image, the streaming creates a trace and erases it while filling it with water. Until now, however, what erased the trace was rather the second signifier, the S_2. In *Identification (Seminar IX)*, it is rather the trait that erases the object, the S_2 that erases the S_1, and the subject appears as -1, elided between the signifiers. Lacan reverses his earlier logic here, emphasising that "it is from their conjunction," i.e. that of the first trait and what erases it, "that a subject" i.e. the cluster, the bouquet, "is constituted" (HB9: 34). Lacan indicates that this requires two times and then distinguishes the notion of erasure (at the heart of his title), the unary trait, the S_1. It is the "blotting-out of no trace whatsoever that might be from before," that is to say that the unary trait establishes the subject by erasing it, by introducing it as pure negativity. Lacan opposes both Derrida and his own construction by which the S_2 was necessary to produce this erasure. The unary trait comes with the letter, it is its effect. The erasure "turns the littoral to terrain" (HB9: 35). It is the symbolic side of the letter, the first half of which is the land side. "Pure *litura* is the littoral" – in other words the letter, in its dimension of pure erasure, is the line of the littoral. "To produce this blotting-out is to reproduce this peerless other half through which the subject subsists," in other words the unary trait, S_1, which represents the subject, without the support of S_2 (which would be the other half of the pair, but which is no longer necessary to the representation of the subject, reproduced by this single half).

"Such is the exploit of calligraphy," notes Lacan (HB9: 35), which is the writing of the unary trait, in that the single brushstroke bears the signature of the calligrapher. Lacan indicates the impossibility for the Westerner to grasp "the point of pressure by which to broach it [the horizontal bar], the suspension by which to halt it." That is to say, the letter does not support itself on a previous primary trace, of which it would be the erasure, but on jouissance. Catching this requires taking a path other than the one the Westerner takes: "It requires a train that you only catch by detaching yourself from whatever might be striking you out" where I understand that the Western train would be the link S_1–S_2 from which it thinks, makes meaning, but the Oriental train only catches itself by detaching itself from any signifying dimension, in order to grasp the jouissance beyond S_1, of that which marks you, as that on which it supports itself.

"Between centre and absence, between knowledge and jouissance, there lies the littoral," notes Lacan, that is to say the S_1, "that only fetches to the literal provided that you are able to take this very same bend at all times"; the littoral turns literal, that is to say it becomes a letter when the object of the impulse that commands repetition is correlated with it.

Gullying and Rupturing of the Semblant

Lacan then specifies that the streaming, the letter, is produced "from between the clouds" (i.e. from the rupture of S_1–S_2). The cloud is an image of the "semblant, par excellence," that is to say of the signifier. "It is from its bursting that comes raining down [...] what was formerly suspended matter" (HB9: 35), that is to say, the letter. He emphasises, moreover, that his vision of streaming is dominated by erasure, which is conjugated at its source, that is to say that the unary trait dominates in the sense that the letter has its source in the rupture of the semblant, of language. "The signifier is no longer presented as an articulation of differential elements," says Leander Pasqual, "that is to say, as a connection of elements that can be isolated. On the contrary, the clouds rather represent the imprecision of form and the inconsistency of the materiality of the signifying chain. This time, the materiality of the signifier becomes the suspended matter."[24] Jacques-Alain Miller points out that Lacan leaves behind, with the meteorological metaphor, the "old mechanics" of the signifier.[25] This rupture, in fact, "dissolves what constituted form," notes Lacan, emphasising that science seeks to pierce the secret of the meteors, but by dismissing jouissance, filth, and life. "What is evoked of jouissance on the breaking of a semblant, this is what presents itself in the real as gullying," says Lacan in opposition to science. The detachment of the S_1, of the unary trait, gullies the real and "evokes" jouissance, in other words, jouissance depends on the signifier, it is attached to the letter that evokes it. If Lacan is interested in the materiality of the signifier with the letter, he does not give consistency to jouissance at all. The gullying is the product of the streaming, or the effect of the letter, under its two faces, real and symbolic, taken on the side of the materiality of language.

According to Lacan, "writing is this very gullying" (HB9: 37). He explains its invocative function of jouissance as follows: "Nothing is more distinct from the void hollowed out by writing than the semblant. The former is a crock ever ready to accommodate jouissance or at the very least invoke it through its artifice" (HB9: 38). Writing is "that which has rained down from the semblant, in so far as it constitutes the signifier" (HB9: 35; in French, this phrase could also be heard as "what is pleasing," *ce qui a plu*), and it is in this sense that it is "in the real, the gullying of the signified," it results from the rupture S_1–S_2, leads towards the outside of meaning and is combined with jouissance.

Lacan opposes the signifier as semblant with the real – "the semblant is what constitutes it" and the real in which the letter operates. This opposition of the real and the semblant is also what distinguishes him from Derrida, against whom Lacan states that writing "does not reproduce" the semblant (Derrida's thesis), but "its language-effects, what is wrought of a language by whosoever speaks it," that is to say that the letter comes under the effects of the subject, it is in the grip of enunciation, the unary trait, and of its second effect, jouissance. "Writing only returns to it on taking a name therefrom," he says: it falls from the semblant but comes closer to it, "returns to it," because of "taking a name;" it retains a signifying face, but with the support of a signifier outside meaning, the S_1 by itself, which is no longer a signifier taken in its differential dimension, of linguistic articulation, but on the edge of the real, and it is in this sense that it is a letter. The S_1 thus becomes a unary trait, the sign of the subject, his name. It takes its name "as happens to these effects among those things that the signifying battery denominates for having enumerated them." The S_1 is an effect of the signifying battery, which is detached from the function of the enumeration, that is, as the subject's number, when it is no longer linked to S_2 to produce meaning.

Writing

To grasp this function of writing, of the letter, of the S_1 taken in its numerical dimension, Lacan evokes effects of writing, of traces: highways, isobars, linked to science, to ciphering, on the one hand, and to the line (to geometry) on the other. He points out that the contemporary architecture of the motorways in Osaka evokes the flight of the bird, that modernity joins ancestral knowledge which had been able to locate the shortest path from one point to another with the help of clouds; in other words, orientation, meaning, is given by the cloud, the semblant. No one follows a straight line spontaneously, not even the path of light, which follows a curve, as Lacan says in the initial lesson of the seminar (XVIII), but the straight line "inscribes something" all the same. Orientation presupposes a geometrical construction. The straight line introduces continuity in a cascade of points, light sticks to its curvature, and the object and the unary trait are combined. Lacan also shows how science deciphers knowledge in the real world, of which it can make an "example" with letters – "our science is only operative by dint of a streaming of devised little letters and graphics." "There can be no straight line except by dint of writing," he notes, "nor metes and bounds except by dint of skyfall" – in other words, semblant and letter, meaning and construction, operate as if they are two indispensable, inescapable and yet distinct dimensions (HB9: 36). He also reminds us that "writing and surveying are artefacts for inhabiting only language"; the letter has a foot in the symbolic, in the semblant, writing inhabits only language, the two are intimately linked. Here too Lacan aims at the limits of a science that would retain a Platonic outlook, the hope of writing all that is real, that the real is rational.

For its part, psychoanalysis teaches that there is no jouissance without the semblant, without meaning, and vice versa. "Beneath the Mirabeau Bridge [...] flows the primal Seine," he says, playing on the equivoque of the streaming that takes place under the bridge of language, but also on the evocation of the

Wolf Man and the primal, repressed and inaccessible scene that Lacan relates here to an effect of writing in the real. He recalls the letter V associated by Freud's patient with the reminiscence of the open wings of a butterfly, which Freud unfolds on the side of castration and on the side of sexual pleasure as well as the construction of fantasy. "But still, one only derives jouissance from it when the word of interpretation rains upon it" (HB9: 36), says Lacan. Interpretation delivers the letter and the jouissance attached to it. The politics of psychoanalysis is that of the symptom, which requires passing through interpretation, something that politics would benefit from learning from, he notes. For all that, he calls for a politics of psychoanalysis that knows how to take advantage of writing, "another account [*parti*] than tribune or a tribunal," no doubt referring to his problems with the IPA. But it is also a question of going beyond the regime of the law, of the Father, to take the support of the materiality of language, which allows us to go beyond the Oedipus, "so that other words might be at play therein, at the cost of our constituting the tribute." I understand here that the analyst in the place of object, of tribute, allows a dimension of speech to be played out other than that of meaning.

"There is no metalanguage," he reminds us, no Other of the Other, no Other of the guarantee of the law, of truth, but the materiality of language, the written word, has just as much guiding force. It can modify that of psychoanalysis. The passage from father to sinthome is already understandable from these lines.

Orienting by the Littoral

"Is it possible to constitute from the littoral a discourse that is characterised by not being oriented by the semblant?" (HB9: 36) Lacan asked as he attempted to do exactly that with the discourse of the analyst. The discourse of the analyst puts the object *a* in the place of the agent, while the other three discourses are oriented by the signifier (S, S_1, S_2). Psychoanalysis must find its orientation in the real, and not in meaning. Its question is identical to that of avant-garde literature, which is "made up of the littoral." This literature proceeds from the letter and not from the semblant, but, for all that, "it substantiates nothing but the break, which only a discourse can produce, with an effect of production." In other words, it can only rely on the letter from its point of rupture from the semblant; nevertheless, it cannot be without a discourse. Lacan uses "discourse" and not "language," because it is from a discourse, from the structure reduced to a few letters, that he locates psychoanalysis and its operation. He emphasises that the letter can be trapped only from the semblant at its rupture, when it gets reduced to a few signifiers. The notion of "substantiation" is also interesting here, since he associates avant-garde literature with science through this term, through which proof moves from truth to reality. The real at stake is that of the letter, which results from this break with the semblant, which is the product of it. It can also be understood here that the letter has an effect of production, of jouissance.

This literature has the ambition "to land on litura-terrain," he states; it is based on the literal and therefore has the ambition "to be ordained by a movement that it calls scientific." One thinks of Oulipo, the acme of this literature.

Lacan, however, marks the divergence, the gap between avant-garde literature and science: "It is a fact that writing has worked wonders here and that everything marks that these wonders are not about to run dry" (does he also think of Lewis Carroll?). His leaning on writing and the letter works wonders here, it summons the reader's jouissance, but it is a matter of knowing how to deal with the object, in the mode of sublimation, whereas Lacan associates science with pollution, like its blind production which ignores itself. By rejecting jouissance, it returns as types of waste, as the death drive.

Predicting the rise of environmental concerns, Lacan announces that science will not be able to last much longer without asking itself what its symptom is. He ironises in passing on the notion of the environment, when it is grasped according to a conception based on a biological approach on a par with that of Uexküll, which is governed by the principle of stimulus and response. For Uexküll, *Umwelt* (environment) would be a reflection of the *Innenwelt* (interior world). They would have common ground. In other words, the mistake is to think in terms of the interaction between man and the environment, that the environment is a reflection of human behaviour ("this is Uexküll's idea behaviourised," HB9: 37), and that it would be enough to improve behaviour to improve the environment (Uexküll's idea "cretinised"), to rely on cognitive-behavioural scientism. This would be to neglect the fact that pollution is a production of science and to persist in the blindness of ignoring jouissance as a product of the semblant, the action of the subject and of the object. Lacan places his hope in an ethics which takes into account knowing how to deal with the symptom and with the object.

He himself wants to "land on lituraterrain," situating himself rather in the wake of contemporary literature. His style is marked by this. He specifies that the image of gullying is not a metaphor, rather "writing is this very gullying." He aims at a littoral style, a use of the concept that is based on the letter and not on the semblant. Jouissance is involved in his work: he "invokes" in his seminar the jouissance of his audience, its accumulation attests to the effect of his seminar. His jouissance is concerned there, as much in the mode of satisfaction – "this keeps me busy" – as much as through the jouissance he deprives himself of. Jouissance is at stake both as lack and as surplus jouissance, on the side of the subject and the Other/other.

A Constellated Sky

Lacan takes up the characteristics of the Japanese language "in as much as writing works it" (HB9: 37) to further clarify what is at stake in the letter. He indicates that a "writing-effect" is attached to the Japanese language. Japanese writing can be read in two different pronunciations: in *on-yomi*, "the character is pronounced distinctly as such," in *kun-yomi*, the character is pronounced according to "what it means" – I'm returning, with regard to Japanese writing, born of a borrowing of its characters from China, hence this double reading, to an article by Jean-Louis Gault.[26]

Lacan invites us to not understand the assemblage of letters constituted by the calligraphic character, such as "the flotsam of the signifier coursing downstream to the rivers of the signified," i.e. the signifier decomposed into phonemes, which are assembled to produce meaning, the signified. "It is the letter as such that provides support for the signifier in keeping with its law of metaphor," he says. Metaphor refers to the law, i.e. to the substitution of signifiers allowed by the articulation of signifiers in the chain, i.e. to the linkage of S_1–S_2. The Japanese language reveals to him that the letter "provides support for the signifier," that is to say that it reveals the autonomy of the letter. The support for the signifier is the conjunction of S_1, the unary trait, and the subject's jouissance. Lacan seems to indicate that this conjunction S_1a becomes autonomous from the articulation S_1–S_2, which he then develops, grasping the particularities of the Japanese subject from the fact of his language. Discourse is that which "ensnares the letter in the net of semblance," that is to say that it ties S_1 and *a* to S_2, thereby producing $\$$.

Lacan avoids thinking in terms of the primacy of the letter, even though it supports the signifier, because it is also caught up in the movement of the discourse, but this does not prevent him from thinking about its autonomy.

The letter is promoted "as a referent that is as essential as every thing" in Japanese discourse, that is to say that it occupies an eminent place there, and that the referent of the discourse is no longer $\$$, but S_1a, the letter, and no longer a subject, "and this changes the status of the subject," says Lacan. If the letter becomes the essential referent of discourse, the subject is situated more on the side of S_1 by itself, in its link to jouissance, and it is in this that it will find itself divided between, on the one hand, the semblants (S_1–S_2), as subject of speech (without recourse to the unary trait alone, it is at this point a subject of pure semblant) and on the other hand of the unary trait and jouissance (S_1a), as a subject of writing. However, the notion of subject is no longer adequate here. What is discovered in "Lituraterre" is part of the movement that will lead to the real unconscious and to the *parlêtre*. The fact that it "draws on a constellated sky and not only on the unary trait for its fundamental identification explains that he can rely only on the Thou, that is to say, in all the grammatical forms of which the slightest statement varies according to the relations of courtesy that it implies in what is signified" (HB9: 37), says Lacan.

Jean-Louis Gault specifies that there is no universal form of shifter in the Japanese language, that is, no "I" that points to a single enunciative source, but some twenty signifiers capable of translating the

"I," in correlation with the "you" that corresponds to it. The "I" is determined by the Other, the "you" to whom he is addressing himself, in his position as a student, son of a wife, master, father, etc. The Japanese subject is strictly based on the Other, "it is relative to the interlocutor," notes Jacques-Alain Miller, "a subject with a de-substantialised status," a subject of pure semblant.[27] It is in this sense that it is based on a constellated sky, an Other that is itself splintered into little others, so that "the variations of truth for reasons of politeness" open "onto a splintered identification" as well. Miller points out that the consequence is that it is based on a constellation of S_1s, a "swarm" of S_1s, "as if, for the Japanese, the basic unary-ness of the trait was missing." Lacan does not dismiss it completely; he specifies that he "draws on a constellated, sky and not only on the unary trait," but he loses himself in the variety of identifications brought about by the predominance of politeness. "Too much support is the same as not having any," says Lacan in the initial conference (this version of "Lituraterre" from *Seminar XVIII* is a little different from that published in *Hurly-Burly*). It is in this sense, says Miller, that Lacan says that in Japan, more than elsewhere, "the truth reinforces the structure of fiction that I denote there, in that this fiction is subject to the laws of politeness." Can we not say that, in a way, the S_1 turns into the S_2, in that the support of the unary trait is masked and lost there? In any case, the subject of speech is dispersed, related to a pure dimension of semblant.

"Oddly enough, this seems to bear the result that there is nothing of the repressed to forbid, since the repressed succeeds in housing itself in the reference to the letter" (HB9: 37), Lacan notes. In order for something to be defended as repressed, the subject has to come to the surface between signifiers, as $, between what it says and what it enounces, but on condition that it does not lack the principle One of the subject's identifications to which its jouissance is correlated. Now this conjunction of the unary trait and jouissance, the letter, becomes the bearer of the repressed and becomes autonomous, does not surface. "In other terms," says Lacan, "the subject is divided as he is everywhere by language, but one of its registers can have its fill of the reference to writing and the other of speech."

The Empire of Semblants

Lacan pays homage to Roland Barthes for having grasped this particularity in his *Empire of Signs*, which is nothing but the "empire of semblants," even though Barthes concludes that "the Japanese subject constitutes an envelope for nothing" (HB9: 38). "The Japanese find this envelope poor,"[28] says Lacan. He distinguishes himself from Barthes by stressing that the latter has precisely misunderstood the dimension of the letter. The "truth" of the Japanese subject, its peculiarity, its specificity, is perhaps to be grasped more from the side of writing than from the side of semblant. "For nothing is more distinct from the void hollowed out by writing than the semblant. The former is a crock ever ready to accommodate jouissance, or at the very least to invoke it through its artifice." Writing indeed furrows a void, but this void welcomes jouissance, it invokes it in the sense of an inescapable call. It invites it, it calls it, but jouissance remains heterogeneous to the dimension of artifice of the semblant. The term "invoke," usually used for a divine figure, also refers to an inexistence in terms of substance or materiality. The Other, at the same time, is still reduced to the object and the One of the unary. The letter is made on one side of an artifice (its symbolic side that borders the semblant), and on its other side from the real, from jouissance.

The Japanese subject communicates nothing of himself, but he hides nothing either, says Lacan. The letter lodges the repressed, the jouissance, the object, but it is autonomous from the subject of pure semblance. Repression is displaced from the signifying chain to the letter; it is in that sense that this subject hides nothing. For all that, it is not reduced to nothing, but identified by the letter. "You are one element amongst others of the ceremonial in which the subject is composed precisely through being able to decompose himself." Can we not also hear that the Other, in a way, is also reduced to the other, caught up in the movement of the signifying chain?

Finally, Lacan evokes the *bunraku*, the puppet theatre, which reveals the structure of the Japanese interlocutory ceremony, where "everything that is said could be read out by a reciter." "Japan is the place where it is utterly natural to support oneself with an interpreter or interpretess, precisely in that it does not necessitate interpretation." In other words, one can support oneself with a simple translator because the approach to the Japanese language does not require interpretation, that is to say, it does not involve equivocation or the subject or interpretation inasmuch as it presupposes that the subject speaks as a subject, as a one ballasted by jouissance. "Tis perpetual translation, made language," Lacan states: to Europeans, perpetual misunderstanding, to Japanese, perpetual translation, because one must not expect from communication any effect of subjective truth that would stop the translation, the parade of meaning, or any quilting point.

With Science?

Thus, Lacan can say that the only communication he encountered in Japan was "scientific communication." He specifies, moreover, that it is the only genuine form of communication, "not being dialogue" (since he puts misunderstanding on the side of Western language). "The latter prompted an eminent biologist to demonstrate his work to me, naturally on the blackboard. The fact that, for want of information, I understood nothing of it does not prevent what remained written up there from being valid." Scientific communication takes place independently of understanding, it is made up of letters written on the blackboard, which convey knowledge that is entirely transmissible, "valid."

For psychoanalysis, Lacan seeks to rely on the model of transmission offered by the mathematical letter, that is to say, outside of meaning and capable of touching the real: "an asceticism of writing seems to me to be admissible only in joining up with *'tis written*," but he specifies a *'tis written* by which "the sexual relation would be established." Let us note the conditional "would be established," if it were written. The sexual relation is that which precisely does not take place with a *'tis written*. Psychoanalysis cannot join science; it is even opposed to it in that psychoanalysis questions a usage of the letter which does not pin down the fact that it is "a crock ever ready to accommodate jouissance." Jacques-Alain Miller, in his essay "Remarques et questions," in *Lacan et la Chose japonaise*, emphasises that "the paradox of science consists in accomplishing a rupture of the semblant without recovering the jouissance that is produced from it," its letters are not those of the calligrapher. "The scientific spirit manifests rather [than the beautiful] the illegible, the difficult to decipher [...] Consequently, one can write scientific knowledge as S_2, write it with a signifying term, even though it is about letters – which makes it possible on occasion to ignore the fact that there is a hole in knowledge." Lacan aims to be inspired by science while at the same time distancing himself from it; rather, with "Lituraterre," he takes the side of art, while pointing out the impasses of science, but also the limits of the asceticism of writing: that which does not cease not to be written, the non-existence of the sexual relation, which will become, in the light of the letter and with it, the compass of the ethics of psychoanalysis.

Translated by Arunava Banerjee

First published as "La condition littorale: lecture de *Lituraterre*", *L'a-graphe*, *Le corps parlant et ses pulsions*, Publication of the Section clinique de Rennes, October 2016, pp. 87-102.

Endnotes

Purloined Picture

1 A point I developed in a previous work: "Le corps féminin de l'Autre," *Quarto*, No. 112-113, 2016, pp. 68-79.

2 Lacan, J., "On a Question Prior to Any Possible Treatment of Psychosis," *Écrits, The First Complete Edition in English*, London/New York, Norton, 2006, p. 485.

3 Lacan, J., *Seminar V, Formations of the Unconscious*, Cambridge, Polity, 2017, p. 132.

4 Miller, J.-A., "Introduction to the Reading of Jacques Lacan's Seminar Anxiety," *Lacanian Ink* 26, Fall 2005, pp. 8-61.

5 Lacan, J., "Le séminaire livre XXII, *R.S.I,* (1974-1975)," text est. by Miller, J.-A., *Ornicar ?* No. 5, lesson of 11 March 1975, p. 17.

6 *Ibid.*

7 Lacan, J., *Seminar XXIII, The Sinthome*, text. est. Miller, J.-A., Cambridge, Polity, 2016.

8 Joyce, J., *Ulysses*, Paris, Shakespeare & Co., 1922.

9 Marret-Maleval, S., "Epiphanies: James Joyce and Virginia Woolf," *Psychoanalytical Notebooks*, No. 9, 2002, pp. 123-142.

10 Marret-Maleval, S., "Reading Joyce," *Hurly-Burly*, No. 4, October 2010, pp. 185-198.

11 Joyce, J., *"Epiphanies," Poems and Shorter Writings*, ed. Ellmann, R., A. Walton Litz, and J. Fergusson, London, Faber & Faber, 1991, p. 162.

12 See Marret-Maleval, S., "Reading Joyce," *op. cit.*

13 "Trésor volé" season 1, episode 3, available online at FranceTV, 2016.

14 Matton, S., *L'homme à la bulle de savon*, Paris, Don Quichotte, 2014, quotes from pp. 27, 33, 76, 40, 42.

15 "Trésor volé" season 1, episode 3.

16 Matton, S., *L'homme à la bulle de savon*, pp. 31, 60.

17 Lacan, L., "Hommage fait à Marguerite Duras du ravissement de Lol V. Stein," *Autres écrits*, Paris, Seuil, 2001, pp. 197, 192.

18 "Trésor volé" season 1, episode 3.

19 Lacan, J., "Le séminaire livre, XXII, *R.S.I,* (1974-1975)," text. est. by Miller, J.-A., *Ornicar ?* No. 5, lesson 11 March 1975, p. 20.

20 "Trésor volé" season 1, episode 3.

21 Matton, S., *op. cit.*, p. 127.

22 "Trésor volé" season 1, episode 3.

23 Interview on Europe 1, available online at europe1, 2014.

24 "Trésor volé," season 1, episode 3.

25 Matton, S., *op. cit.*, p. 234.

26 "Trésor volé" season 1, episode 3.

27 Joyce, J., *A Portrait of the Artist as a Young Man*, London, Grafton, 1916.

Love and Transference

1 Lacan, J., Le Séminaire, XXI, Les non-dupes errent, 19 March 1974, unpublished.

2 Lacan, J., "P*resentation on Transference," Écrits: The First Complete Edition in English*, London/New York, Norton, 2006, pp. 183-184.

3 Lacan, J., *Transference, The Seminar of Jacques Lacan, Book VIII*, text. est. Miller, J.-A., Cambridge, Polity, 2015.

4 Lacan, J., *Encore, On Feminine Sexuality, the Limits of Love and Knowledge: The Seminar of Jacques Lacan, Book XX* (1972-1973), text. est. Miller, J.-A., New York: Norton, 1998, 5, 3, 44, 126, 45.

5 Miller, J.-A., "Six Paradigms of Jouissance", *Psychoanalytical Notebooks*, No. 34, 2019, pp. 63-64.

6 Lacan, J., ... *or Worse: The Seminar of Jacques Lacan, Book XIX*, text. est. Miller, J.-A., Cambridge, Polity, 2018, Ch. 5, Ch. 10.

7 Miller, J.-A., "Le partenaire symptôme," *L'orientation lacanienne* (annual course delivered with the framework of the Department of Psychoanalysis, University of Paris 8, lesson of 25 March 1998, unpublished).

8 Lacan, J., *Le Séminaire, XXI*, *op. cit.*

9 Lacan, J., *Seminar XXIV, L'insu que sait de l'une bévue s'aile à mourre*, lesson of 21 December 1976, unpublished.

Littoral Condition

1 Lacan, J., "Lituraterre," Hurly-Burly, No. 9, 2013, pp. 29-38.

2 Lacan, J., "The Instance of the Letter in the Unconscious, or Reason Since Freud," *Écrits, The First Complete Edition in English*, New York/London, Norton, 2006.

3 Miller, J.-A., "Six Paradigms of Jouissance," *Psychoanalytical Notebooks*, No. 34, 2019, pp. 11-77.

4 Carroll, L., *Sylvie and Bruno*, in *The Penguin Complete Lewis Carroll*, Harmondsworth, Penguin Books, 1983.

5 Miller, J.-A., *L'orientation lacanienne*, class of 16 May 2007, published online in *Ten Line News*, No. 330, 20 May 2007 (in French); see World Association of Psychoanalysis website.

6 Lacan, J., "Hommage rendu à Lewis Carroll," read out on 31 December 1966, on the radio channel France Culture, with the title "Commentaire d'un psychan-alyste." Transcription by Marlène Bélilos from the soundtrack. Text established by Jacques-Alain Miller in *Ornicar ?* No. 50, Navarin-Seuil, 2002.

7 Lacan, J., "Hommage fait à Marguerite Duras du ravissement de Lol V. Stein" (1965), in *Autres écrits*, Paris, Seuil, 2001, p. 197.

8 Bonaparte, M., *Edgar Poe, sa vie, son oeuvre*, Paris, Denoël et Steele, 1933. Marie Bonaparte interprets the tribulations of a narrator in a super-natural land in terms of little Edgar's Oedipus complex and primitive scene. "But the deep meaning of this sinister tale lies in the fate of Usher.

Poe is punished for being unfaithful to his mother in loving Madelina-Virginia. Usher-Poe is punished for not having dared to seek out and win back the mother of his childhood when, like Annabel Lee, men took her away, and for having then kept silent and resigned himself to his infantile misunderstanding of death. Usher-Poe is punished for his sadism, of which Roderick's behaviour towards his sister bears witness. Finally, Usher-Poe is punished for having nurtured incestuous infantile desires for his mother."

9 The carnivalesque is a reversal of values, an undermining of the fixity of meaning, an escape from official values.

10 "Dialogueism, in Bakhtin's sense, is about discourse in general. It designates the forms of the presence of the other in discourse: discourse in fact emerges only in a process of interaction between an individual consciousness and another, which inspires it and to which it responds." Laurent Jenny, "Méthodes et problèmes: dialogisme et polyphonie," training document of the University of Geneva,

11 Derrida J., *The Postcard: From Socrates to Freud and Beyond*, Chicago, University of Chicago Press, 1987.

12 Pasqual, L., "Usages cliniques de la lettre, du bien-dire au savoir-lire," doctoral thesis supervised by Sophie Marret-Maleval, defended at University of Paris 8, January 2016, p. 215.

13 Miller, J.-A., "De la nature des semblants" (1991-1992), *L'orientation lacanienne* (annual course delivered within the framework of the Department of Psychoanalysis, University of Paris 8, lesson of 22 January 1992, unpublished.)

14 Laurent, É., "The Purloined Letter and the Tao of the Psychoanalyst," *Hurly-Burly*, No. 9, 2019, pp. 51-77. Also *The Later Lacan: An Introduction*, ed. V. Voruz and B. Wolf, Albany, State University of New York Press, 2007, pp. 25-52.

15 A *peluche* is a teddy bear or a soft cuddly toy. See note 20.

16 Marret-Maleval, S., "Le corps féminin de l'Autre," *Quarto*, No. 112-13, May 2016.

17 Lacan, J., *Le séminaire livre XVIII, D'un discours qui ne serait pas du semblant* (1971), text est. Miller, J.-A., Paris, Seuil, 2006, p. 118.

18 Laurent, É., "The purloined ...", *op. cit.*, pp. 57-8.

19 Lacan, J., "The Subversion of the Subject and the Dialectic of Desire in the Freudian Unconscious," *Ecrits, op. cit.*, p. 696.

20 Beatrice Khiara-Foxton and Adrian Price translated these words as Nomorenone, and Cuddly-Hun-to-Boot for the *Hurly-Burly* edition of "Lituraterre," with the following note: "Papeludun is loosely homophonic with 'pas plus d'un', 'not more than one' but is also evocative of 'papelard', an informal term for 'paper' that incorporates the Catalan word *papel. un-en-Peluce*, is loosely homophonic with *un en plus*, "one more," or "an extra one". As in English, *hun* in French evokes an aggressive invader, but is also reminiscent of the *Hún* cloud-soul in Chinese thought ("Hun and Po" soul duality). *En-Peluce* resembles *en-peluche*, the suffix added to an animal name or character to indicate that it is a stuffed "cuddly" toy. See footnotes 13 and 14, p. 34 (HB9: 34).

21 The French verb *appuyer* carries the meanings of both to support and to create in this context.

22 "que l'habite qui parle"
foreshadows a similar pun the
following year in *L'étourdit* : labiter.
[*Autres écrits*, Paris, Seuil, 2001,
p. 474] where the reader can also
hear *la bite*, a vulgar term for penis,
note translators Khiara-Foxton
and Price in (HB9: 33).

23 Lacan, J., *Le séminaire livre XVIII*,
op. cit., p. 120.

24 Pasqual, L., "Usages cliniques ...,"
op. cit., p. 213.

25 Miller, J.-A., "De la nature des
semblants," *L'orientation lacanienne*
(annual course delivered within the
framework of the Department of
Psychoanalysis, University of Paris 8,
lesson of 15 April 1992, unpublished.)

26 Gault, J.-L., "Quelques traits
remarquables de la langue japonaise," *Lacan et la Chose japonaise*,
Paris, Navarin, 1988, pp. 21-35.

27 Miller, J.-A., "Remarques et
questions," *Lacan et la Chose
japonaise*, Navarin, 1988, pp. 98, 102.

28 i.e. the Japanese did not
appreciate Barthes's remark.

Individual or institutional online purchases
can be made from our website:

www.londonsociety-nls.org.uk

CPSIA information can be obtained
at www.ICGtesting.com
Printed in the USA
LVHW080412101122
732756LV00004B/214

9 781916 157620